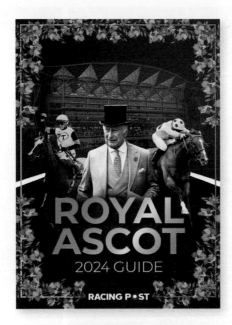

Editor **NICK PULFORD**

Designed by David Dew

Cover designed by Duncan Olner

Contributors

Richard Birch	David Jennings	Tom Segal
Mark Brown	Kevin Morley	Craig Thake
Matt Gardner	Graeme Rodway	Nick Watts
Jack Haynes	Stefan Searle	Richard Young

With grateful thanks to Ascot Racecourse for their invaluable assistance

Published in 2024 by Pitch Publishing on behalf of Racing Post, 9 Donnington Park, 85 Birdham Road, Chichester, West Sussex PO20 7AJ. www.pitchpublishing.co.uk info@pitchpublishing.co.uk

Pitch Publishing specifies that post-press changes may occur to any information given in this publication. A catalogue record for this book is available from the British Library.

ISBN 978-1839501487
Printed in Great Britain by Short Run Press

CHANGING TIMES

Editor Nick Pulford outlines the tweaks at Royal Ascot 2024

Changes are afoot at Royal Ascot this year but, have no fear, the traditions that have underpinned the famous occasion for centuries will remain intact.

From the royal procession to the bandstand singalong, the cherished elements of a special day at the royal meeting will follow a familiar pattern. At the heart, of course, will be a feast of top-class racing spread across five days and 35 events.

Some tweaks will be in evidence, however. With this year's meeting clashing with the Euro 2024 football – which kicks off four days before Royal Ascot – there has been a reshuffle of race orders and start times to maximise coverage on ITV1 where possible.

On each day the programme gets under way at the traditional start time of 2.30pm, but from the third race onwards the race times are five minutes later than before.

On Wednesday and Thursday, when ITV1 is showing a 2pm Euro match, the televised racing will start on ITV4 and switch to the main channel for the day's feature race, fourth on the card at 4.25.

On Friday and Saturday, the racing will start on ITV1 and the feature race will be third on the card at 3.45, before the main channel switches over to football and the last four races are shown on ITV4.

Tuesday has the same tweaks to race times so that the entire week follows the same pattern but the first six races will be on ITV1 (with the last on ITV4) as the channel is showing no football that day.

There is a significant change on Tuesday, however, with the Group 1 sprint (known as the King's Stand Stakes since 1901) renamed the King Charles III Stakes in honour of the new monarch.

On Wednesday the Kensington Palace Stakes has been switched to the straight course following feedback from jockeys, owners and trainers about the congestion that occurred from having a 20-runner handicap on the Old Mile. The Duke of Cambridge Stakes moves the other way to maintain the balance of round/straight races.

Ascot has also taken steps to ensure the royal meeting remains attractive not only for its traditions but also as a global race meeting. Prize-money has increased to a record total of £10m, with the Group 1s ranging in value from £650,000 to £1m and a minimum £110,000 for the lesser races.

With a galaxy of stars set to light up the track, racing fans will be the winners.

ROYAL ASCOT ESSENTIALS

DATES

- Royal Ascot 2024 takes place over five days from Tuesday June 18 to Saturday June 22

TICKETS

- **Royal Enclosure** Available only to members and their guests, or non-members with a hospitality guest day badge
- **Queen Anne Enclosure** £90 Tuesday & Wednesday, £99 Thursday-Saturday
- **Village Enclosure** £85 Thursday-Saturday
- **Windsor Enclosure** £49 Tuesday & Wednesday, £65 Thursday-Saturday

BY CAR

- **From London & the North** M4 Junction 6 onto the A332 Windsor bypass and follow the signs to Ascot
- **From the West** M4 Junction 10 to the A329(M) signed to Bracknell and follow the signs to Ascot
- **From the South & East** M3 Junction 3 onto the A332 signed to Bracknell and follow the signs to Ascot
- **From the Midlands** M40 southbound, Junction 4. Take the A404 towards the M4 (Junction 8/9). On the M4 head towards Heathrow/London. Leave M4 at Junction 6 and follow the A332 Windsor bypass to Ascot
- More than 8,000 car parking spaces are available and pre-booking is advised. Car Park 8 costs £40 per day

BY TRAIN

- South Western Railway runs a frequent service to Ascot from Reading, Guildford and London Waterloo. The average journey time is 27 minutes from Reading and 52 minutes from Waterloo. The railway station is a seven-minute walk from the racecourse

TV DETAILS

- All 35 races will be broadcast live on ITV, with 30 hours of live coverage across the week. The Opening Show preview programme will be shown daily at 9am on ITV4 and coverage of the racing will start at 1.30pm
- Sky Sports Racing will also broadcast live from Ascot on each of the five days

ITV COVERAGE

Tuesday
2.30 Queen Anne Stakes (Group 1) ITV1
3.05 Coventry Stakes (Group 2) ITV1
3.45 King Charles III Stakes (Group 1) ITV1
4.25 St James's Palace Stakes (Group 1) ITV1
5.05 Ascot Stakes (Handicap) ITV1
5.40 Wolferton Stakes (Listed) ITV1
6.15 Copper Horse Stakes (Handicap) ITV4

Wednesday
2.30 Queen Mary Stakes (Group 2) ITV4
3.05 Queen's Vase (Group 2) ITV4
3.45 Duke of Cambridge Stakes (Group 2) ITV4
4.25 Prince of Wales's Stakes (Group 1) ITV1
5.05 Royal Hunt Cup (Heritage Handicap) ITV1
5.40 Kensington Palace Stakes (Handicap) ITV1
6.15 Windsor Castle Stakes (Listed) ITV4

Thursday
2.30 Norfolk Stakes (Group 2) ITV4
3.05 King George V Stakes (Handicap) ITV4
3.45 Ribblesdale Stakes (Group 2) ITV4
4.25 Gold Cup (Group 1) ITV1
5.05 Britannia Stakes (Heritage Handicap) ITV1
5.40 Hampton Court Stakes (Group 3) ITV1
6.15 Buckingham Palace Stakes (Handicap) ITV4

Friday
2.30 Albany Stakes (Group 3) ITV1
3.05 Commonwealth Cup (Group 1) ITV1
3.45 Coronation Stakes (Group 1) ITV1
4.25 Duke of Edinburgh Stakes (Handicap) ITV4
5.05 Sandringham Stakes (Handicap) ITV4
5.40 King Edward VII Stakes (Group 2) ITV4
6.15 Palace of Holyroodhouse Stakes (Handicap) ITV4

Saturday
2.30 Chesham Stakes (Listed) ITV1
3.05 Hardwicke Stakes (Group 2) ITV1
3.45 Queen Elizabeth II Jubilee Stakes (Group 1) ITV1
4.25 Jersey Stakes (Group 3) ITV4
5.05 Wokingham Stakes (Heritage Handicap) ITV4
5.40 Golden Gates Stakes (Handicap) ITV4
6.15 Queen Alexandra Stakes (Conditions) ITV4

DAY ONE

A new name appears on Royal Ascot's opening day, which features the traditional three Group 1s in the first four races to get the week under way in a blaze of big-race action.

The middle leg of the Group 1 blitz, long known as the King's Stand Stakes, has been renamed the King Charles III Stakes in honour of the new monarch, who had a successful first Royal Ascot on the throne last year when Desert Hero won the King George V Handicap in the royal colours.

The other slight tweak to the programme is that the race times are five minutes later than before from the third race onwards, as they are on each day of this year's meeting.

The established curtain-raiser is the Queen Anne Stakes down the straight course for the older elite milers. Often it is a major stepping stone to championship honours but recent runnings have produced a number of shocks, including last year's 33-1 winner Triple Time.

Third on the card is the King Charles III, which goes off at 3.45. The big five-furlong sprint has taken on an international flavour in the 21st century and Australia is set to have a strong presence again with exciting speedsters Chain Of Lightning and Asfoora.

The third Group 1 of the day is the St James's Palace Stakes, which brings together the top three-year-old milers for a showdown on the round course and is another championship pointer.

Last year's race went to Paddington, who had already won the Irish 2,000 Guineas and went on to land the Eclipse and Sussex Stakes.

The main race among the supporting cast is the Group 2 Coventry Stakes, renowned as the premier race for two-year-old colts at the meeting. Among last year's field were subsequent Group 1 winner Bucanero Fuerte (third) and this year's 2,000 Guineas third Haatem (fifth).

The day's main handicap is the Ascot Stakes over the marathon trip of two and a half miles. This has become a major target for the top jumps trainers as well as the big Flat stables, with victory last year going to Nicky Henderson with Ahorsewithnoname.

Next comes the Wolferton Stakes, a Listed race over a mile and a quarter for four-year-olds and upwards, while staying handicappers also round off the day in the Copper Horse Stakes over a mile and three-quarters.

Tuesday June 18

2.30 **Queen Anne Stakes** (Group 1) Last year's winner: Triple Time 33-1	**1m** 4yo+	£750,000
3.05 **Coventry Stakes** (Group 2) Last year's winner: River Tiber 11-8f	**6f** 2yo	£175,000
3.45 **King Charles III Stakes** (Group 1) Last year's winner: Bradsell 14-1	**5f** 3yo+	£650,000
4.25 **St James's Palace Stakes** (Group 1) Last year's winner: Paddington 11-5	**1m** 3yo colts	£650,000
5.05 **Ascot Stakes** (Handicap) Last year's winner: Ahorsewithnoname 7-1	**2m4f** 4yo+	£110,000
5.40 **Wolferton Stakes** (Listed) Last year's winner: Royal Champion 16-1	**1m2f** 4yo+	£120,000
6.15 **Copper Horse Stakes** (Handicap) Last year's winner: Vauban Evensf	**1m6f** 4yo+	£110,000

Race value is total prize-money

Story of the last ten years

	FORM	WINNER	AGE & WGT	Adj RPR	SP	TRAINER	BEST RPR LAST 12 MONTHS (RUNS SINCE)
23	1/17-	**Triple Time** D	4 9-2	124-14	33-1	Kevin Ryan	won Superior Mile Gp3 (1m) (1)
22	111-1	**Baaeed** CD	4 9-2	141T	1-6f	William Haggas	won Lockinge Stakes Gp1 (1m) (0)
21	13-11	**Palace Pier** C, D	4 9-0	141T	2-7f	John & Thady Gosden	won Lockinge Stakes Gp1 (1m) (0)
20	2714-	**Circus Maximus** C, D, BF	4 9-0	133-3	4-1f	Aidan O'Brien (IRE)	won Prix du Moulin Gp1 (1m) (1)
19	66-30	**Lord Glitters** CD	6 9-0	132-4	14-1	David O'Meara	3rd Dubai Turf Gp1 (1m1f) (1)
18	48-36	**Accidental Agent** C	4 9-0	127-10	33-1	Eve Johnson Houghton	won Ascot Class 2 hcap (7f) (4)
17	12-31	**Ribchester** C, D	4 9-0	139T	11-10f	Richard Fahey	won Lockinge Stakes Gp1 (1m) (0)
16	-1111	**Tepin** D	5 8-11	138T	11-2	Mark Casse (CAN)	won Keeneland Gd1 (1m½f) (1)
15	1-111	**Solow** D	5 9-0	139-2	11-8f	Freddy Head (FR)	won Dubai Turf Gp1 (1m1f) (1)
14	4216-	**Toronado** C, D	4 9-0	143T	4-5f	Richard Hannon	won Sussex Stakes Gp1 (1m) (1)

WINS-PL-RUNS 4yo 7-10-55, 5yo 2-7-38, 6yo+ 1-2-30 **FAVOURITES** £3.73

TRAINERS IN THIS RACE (w-pl-r) Aidan O'Brien 1-4-12, Richard Hannon 1-0-12, John & Thady Gosden 1-1-2, William Haggas 1-2-4, Kevin Ryan 1-0-3, Roger Varian 0-1-7, Saeed Bin Suroor 0-1-3, Francis Graffard 0-0-1, Karl Burke 0-0-1

FATE OF FAVOURITES 1121001114 **POSITION OF WINNER IN MARKET** 1131061119

Triple Time leads the charge for home in last year's Queen Anne Stakes

2.30 Queen Anne Stakes

FIRST run in 1840, the Queen Anne Stakes commemorates the monarch who established racing at Ascot and is the meeting's top mile race for older horses (aged four and up).

Last year's winner
The four-year-old Triple Time fitted the age and distance criteria but broke every other key trend as he came back from an injury-interrupted previous season and a near nine-month absence to score for Kevin Ryan at 33-1, beating 11-4 shot Inspiral by a neck.

Form Eight of the last ten winners came into the race with an adjusted Racing Post Rating of at least 132 and seven already had Group 1 success on their record. The two who did not fit either pattern were Accidental Agent (2018) and Triple Time, although the former had run in a Group 1 last time (sixth in the Lockinge) and the latter had been due to run in the Lockinge but was withdrawn on raceday.

Key races The Lockinge is the main stepping stone – Triple Time is the only one of the last 12 British-trained winners of the Queen Anne not to have run in the Newbury Group 1 (the other 11 finished 82411116011). Two of Aidan O'Brien's last three winners also prepped in the Lockinge (finishing 65).

Of the last 17 winners, only Triple Time and the US-trained Tepin (2016) had not run at the top level last time (they had competed in Group/Grade 2) – the three French-trained winners had all run in the Prix d'Ispahan. Often the previous year's Guineas and Royal Ascot results are a good sign of the right quality. Half of the 18 four-year-old winners since 2000 had secured a top-three finish in a Guineas (three won) or in the St James's Palace Stakes (four won). Most of the other four-year-old winners were late developers or had been held up by injury the previous year (Triple Time was in that category).

Trainers
In recent years the yards to note have been Ballydoyle and the Hannon stable. Since 2008 with fancied runners (below 10-1) the form figures for O'Brien are 1662129518 and for the Hannons they are 1211546. The recent French record is good, with three wins and five places from 18 runners since 2005.

Betting There have been eight successful favourites in the last 13 runnings but Triple Time was the third big upset in recent years, following Accidental Agent (33-1) and Lord Glitters (14-1) in 2018 and 2019. Before them, the last winner from outside the top four in the betting was Refuse To Bend (12-1) in 2004.

FIRST run in 1890, this is the most valuable race for juveniles at Royal Ascot and the season's first high-class contest for the age group, regularly proving a stepping stone to Group 1 level.

Last year's winner River Tiber was a near perfect fit on trends (falling just short on distance, having won at 5½f) and justified 11-8 favouritism to give Aidan O'Brien his tenth win in this race, albeit by just a neck from 20-1 shot Army Ethos.

Form One run is often enough to prepare for this test, as it was for ten winners in the past 20 years (only three winners in that period had run more than twice). All but one of those once-raced juveniles had won, and indeed just five of the last 20 winners had suffered a defeat before Ascot. The only winner this century to arrive

Key trends
▸ *Won last time out, 9/10*
▸ *No more than three starts, 9/10*
▸ *Won a previous start by at least two lengths, 8/10*
▸ *Rated within 7lb of RPR top-rated, 7/10 (exceptions 13lb to 22lb off top)*
▸ *Adjusted RPR of at least 110, 7/10*
▸ *Distance winner, 6/10*

Other factors
▸ *Seven winners were undefeated. Buratino, who won in 2015, had been beaten twice over 5f but was undefeated over 6f*
▸ *The market had usually been a strong indicator but three of the last seven winners were priced in at least double figures*

off the back of a last-time-out defeat was 150-1 shot Nando Parrado in 2020.

Key races Southern-trained contenders often start in a Newmarket or Newbury maiden/novice; York is a good route for a northern challenger; in Ireland, check the Curragh and Leopardstown. Three of the last ten winners made their debut on the all-weather. Only one of the last ten winners had competed in Pattern company (winning the Listed Marble Hill Stakes at the Curragh).

Trainers Aidan O'Brien is the top trainer with ten victories since his first with Harbour Master in 1997 (seven of the ten were favourite). Look out for Archie Watson – he has had only five Coventry runners but the three most fancied (up to 20-1) finished 312.

Betting Market position is a good guide, with 16 of the last 20 winners in the first four in the betting.

Story of the last ten years

FORM	WINNER	AGE & WGT	Adj RPR	SP	TRAINER	BEST RPR LAST 12 MONTHS (RUNS SINCE)
23 11	**River Tiber**	2 9-3	118T	11-8f	Aidan O'Brien (IRE)	won Navan maiden (5½f) (1)
22 1	**Bradsell** D	2 9-3	111-7	8-1	Archie Watson	won York Class 3 novice (6f) (0)
21 1	**Berkshire Shadow**	2 9-1	102-14	11-1	Andrew Balding	won Newbury Class 4 maiden (5f) (0)
20 5	**Nando Parrado**	2 9-1	81-22	150-1	Clive Cox	5th Newmarket Class 5 maiden (6f) (0)
19 21	**Arizona** D	2 9-1	111T	15-8f	Aidan O'Brien (IRE)	won Curragh maiden (6f) (0)
18 1	**Calyx** D	2 9-1	115-2	2-1f	John Gosden	won Newmarket Class 4 novice (6f) (0)
17 1	**Rajasinghe** D	2 9-1	103-13	11-1	Richard Spencer	won Newcastle Class 4 novice (6f) (0)
16 11	**Caravaggio**	2 9-1	119T	13-8f	Aidan O'Brien (IRE)	won Curragh Listed (5f) (0)
15 13121	**Buratino** D	2 9-1	118T	6-1	Mark Johnston	won Woodcote Stakes Listed (6f) (0)
14 1	**The Wow Signal** D	2 9-1	110-4	5-1j	John Quinn	won Ayr Class 4 maiden (6f) (0)

FAVOURITES £3.88 **TRAINERS IN THIS RACE** (w-pl-r) Aidan O'Brien 3-3-16, Archie Watson 1-2-5, Andrew Balding 1-0-3, Clive Cox 1-0-7, Jim Bolger 0-0-1, Charlie Appleby 0-0-5, Richard Hannon 0-4-16, Wesley Ward 0-0-4, John & Thady Gosden 0-0-2

FATE OF FAVOURITES 1014110641 **POSITION OF WINNER IN MARKET** 1316110641

IRISH CHAMPIONS FESTIVAL

**Leopardstown & The Curragh
14th & 15th September 2024**

2 incredible days of
world-class racing
and entertainment

IT ALL
COMES DOWN
TO THIS

TICKETS ON SALE NOW

For your best weekend package visit
irishchampionsfestival.ie

FIRST run in 1860, this five-furlong contest is the fastest race of the week, usually completed in less than a minute. Having been a Group 2 for 20 years, the race regained Group 1 status in 2008. Long known as the King's Stand Stakes, it has been renamed this year as the King Charles III Stakes.

Last year's winner
Bradsell broke the key trends on RPR but otherwise was a good fit with his 14-1 success, achieving the remarkable feat of adding this prize to his Coventry win 12 months earlier.

Form Group 1-winning form is important with overseas raiders (all five Australian winners and Lady Aurelia qualified, with Hong Kong's Little Bridge an exception) but not so much for the British and Irish (five of the last ten were scoring for the first time at this level). A good level of Group form is virtually a must, however.

Four of the last ten winners were top on adjusted Racing Post Ratings and Bradsell is the only winner in the past decade who was more than 7lb off top (that measure is usually a good way to narrow the field).

Key races Five of the last ten winners from Britain and Ireland had contested the Palace House Stakes at Newmarket or the Temple Stakes at Haydock (and

Story of the last ten years

FORM		WINNER	AGE & WGT	Adj RPR	SP	TRAINER	BEST RPR LAST 12 MONTHS (RUNS SINCE)
23	14-33	**Bradsell** C	3 9-1	118^{-17}	14-1	Archie Watson	3rd Commonwealth Cup Trial Gp3 (6f) (1)
22	1-231	**Nature Strip** D	7 9-7	133^T	9-4	Chris Waller (AUS)	won TJ Smith Stakes Gp1 (6f) (0)
21	5-723	**Oxted** BF	5 9-5	129^{-3}	4-1	Roger Teal	won July Cup Gp1 (6f) (4)
20	2110-	**Battaash** D, BF	6 9-4	139^T	5-6f	Charlie Hills	won Nunthorpe Stakes Gp1 (5f) (1)
19	3-111	**Blue Point** CD	5 9-4	133^{-6}	5-2	Charlie Appleby	won Al Quoz Sprint Gp1 (6f) (0)
18	41-29	**Blue Point** C	4 9-4	131^{-7}	6-1	Charlie Appleby	2nd Meydan Gp2 (5f) (1)
17	113-1	**Lady Aurelia** CD	3 8-9	138^T	7-2	Wesley Ward (USA)	won Keeneland Listed (5½f) (0)
16	05-11	**Profitable** D	4 9-4	131^{-3}	4-1	Clive Cox	won Temple Stakes Gp2 (5f) (0)
15	42-17	**Goldream** CD	6 9-4	125^{-6}	20-1	Robert Cowell	won Palace House Stakes Gp3 (5f) (1)
14	2-471	**Sole Power** CD	7 9-4	130^T	5-1	Eddie Lynam (IRE)	won King's Stand Stakes Gp1 (5f) (7)

WINS-PL-RUNS 3yo 2-3-20, 4yo 2-8-46, 5yo 2-5-37, 6yo+ 4-4-51 **FAVOURITES** -£8.17

TRAINERS IN THIS RACE (w-pl-r) Archie Watson 1-1-2, Charlie Hills 1-4-10, Clive Cox 1-1-7, Wesley Ward 1-0-4, Karl Burke 0-0-2, Henry Candy 0-1-3, Aidan O'Brien 0-0-9, William Haggas 0-1-3, Richard Hannon 0-0-2, Andrew Balding 0-0-4

FATE OF FAVOURITES 3503021402 **POSITION OF WINNER IN MARKET** 3822321225

3.45 King Charles III Stakes

Bradsell wins last year's race at 14-1 for Archie Watson

Key trends

▶ *Adjusted RPR of at least 125, 9/10*
▶ *Rated within 7lb of RPR top-rated, 9/10*
▶ *Ran at least twice that season, 8/10*
▶ *Drawn seven or higher, 8/10*
▶ *Group winner over 5f, 7/10*
▶ *Won that season, 6/10*

Other factors

▶ *In 2020, Battaash was the first successful favourite since Scenic Blast in 2009*
▶ *Five beaten favourites had won a Group race last time*
▶ *The record of Palace House winners is 1113340*

Longest-priced winners
Squander Bug (1948) & Don't Worry Me (1997), 33-1

Shortest-priced winner
Lochsong 3-10 (1994)

Most successful trainer
5 wins: **Vincent O'Brien**
Cassarate (1952), Abergwaun (1973), Godswalk (1977), Solinus (1978), Bluebird (1987)

Most successful jockey
7 wins: **Lester Piggott**
Right Boy (1957), Majority Rule (1963), Swing Easy (1971), Abergwaun (1973), Godswalk (1977), Solinus (1978), Never So Bold (1985)

*All figures since 1946

frequently both) that season and four of them had won at least one of those contests (the other was third) – a win in the Palace House seems to count for more, with five of the last ten to attempt the double having been successful (compared with only one of the last 13 Temple winners to try). The Abernant Stakes at Newmarket, Sandy Lane Stakes at Haydock and Duke of York Stakes at York have also been stepping stones to success recently. Significant races from further afield are the Prix du Gros-Chene (The Tatling in 2004, Equiano in 2008 and Prohibit in 2011 all placed before coming here) and the Prix de Saint-Georges, won by French-trained Chineur before his King's Stand

victory in 2005 (Prohibit fourth in 2011).

Trainers As well as top-level international trainers, the roll of honour includes several noted for their handling of sprinters – Robert Cowell (Prohibit in 2011 and Goldream in 2015), Eddie Lynam (Sole Power in 2013 and 2014), Clive Cox (Profitable in 2016) and Archie Watson (Bradsell last year).

Betting Only three of the last 29 favourites have won but the market is still a good guide. Since Choisir's 25-1 breakthrough for Australia in 2003, at a time when the strength of their challenge was underestimated, 16 of the 20 winners have been no bigger than 8-1 and 13 of those came from the top three in the betting.

DAY ONE

FIRST run in 1834, this mile contest for three-year-old colts is the third Group 1 of the opening day and often features a clash between the Guineas combatants in Britain, France and Ireland.

Last year's winner

Paddington was a perfect fit on the trends, following on from his Irish 2,000 Guineas success to score here at 11-5, easily beating the Newmarket Guineas winner Chaldean (13-8 favourite).

Form Guineas form is key. Paddington was the 21st winner in the last 24 runnings to have run in at least one Guineas and he was the 16th of those 21 to have enjoyed Classic success (some had done so in more than one of them). Four more had been runner-up, with the worst position being Excellent Art's fourth in the French Guineas in 2007.

Key races Twelve of the last 24 winners had run in both the Newmarket and Irish Guineas and Poetic Flare in 2021 was only the third of those to go backwards on the second run in terms of their finishing position (Zafeen was 14th in Ireland after being runner-up at Newmarket in 2003 and Galileo Gold went from first to second in 2016). Of the seven who did not win at Newmarket, four stepped up to first place in Ireland.

Three of the last 14 winners – Canford Cliffs (2010), Kingman (2014) and Barney Roy (2017) – reversed form here after a Guineas defeat at Newmarket. The first two of those had preceded Ascot success with Guineas victory in Ireland, while Barney Roy had not run in between. Mastercraftsman in 2009 also reversed Newmarket form with the best performer from that Classic (winner Sea The Stars did not run at Ascot, having gone on to win the Derby instead).

Trainers Not surprisingly, given his tremendous strength in depth in the Classics division, Aidan O'Brien has won nine of the last 24 runnings. Between them, his nine winners had

run in 14 Guineas with form figures of 22611141151111 – six of them had won a Guineas and three had done the Newmarket/Irish Guineas double.

Betting The preponderance of strong Guineas form means favourites have a good record, with 14 winning in the 24 runnings since 2000. No winner has been bigger than 10-1 in that period and only one (Circus Maximus) came from outside the top four in the betting. The last shock winner was Brief Truce at 25-1 in 1992.

Aidan O'Brien in the winner's enclosure after Paddington's success 12 months ago

Key trends

▸ *From the first three in the market, 9/10*

▸ *Rated within 7lb of RPR top-rated, 8/10 (six were top-rated)*

▸ *Had won or placed in a Group 1, 7/10*

▸ *Adjusted RPR of at least 132, 7/10*

▸ *Had finished in the first three in a 2,000 Guineas, 7/10*

Other factors

▸ *Winners who had run in a Guineas finished 211211 at Newmarket and 11221 at the Curragh. The 2021*

winner Poetic Flare also ran in the French Guineas (sixth) – the first since Excellent Art in 2007 (fourth)

▸ *Four winners had run in the British and Irish Guineas, with all making the frame in both*

▸ *Without Parole in 2018 and Palace Pier in 2020 (both trained by John Gosden) are the only two winners not to have run in a Group 1 that season since Shavian in 1990*

▸ *Aidan O'Brien has won nine of the last 24 runnings*

4.25 St James's Palace Stakes

Story of the last ten years

FORM	WINNER	AGE & WGT	Adj RPR	SP	TRAINER	BEST RPR LAST 12 MONTHS (RUNS SINCE)
23 1-111	**Paddington** D	3 9-2	132^T	11-5	Aidan O'Brien (IRE)	won Irish 2,000 Guineas Gp1 (1m) (0)
22 121-1	**Coroebus** D	3 9-2	135^T	10-11f	Charlie Appleby	won 2,000 Guineas Gp1 (1m) (0)
21 -1162	**Poetic Flare** D	3 9-0	134^T	7-2f	Jim Bolger (IRE)	won 2,000 Guineas Gp1 (1m) (2)
20 11-1	**Palace Pier** D	3 9-0	127^{-15}	4-1	John Gosden	won Newcastle Class 2 hcap (1m) (0)
19 34-16	**Circus Maximus** D	3 9-0	126^{-13}	10-1	Aidan O'Brien (IRE)	4th Futurity Trophy Gp1 (1m) (2)
18 1-11	**Without Parole** D	3 9-0	128^{-7}	9-4f	John Gosden	won Yarmouth Class 5 novice (1m) (1)
17 1-12	**Barney Roy** C, D	3 9-0	132^{-7}	5-2	Richard Hannon	2nd 2,000 Guineas Gp1 (1m) (0)
16 13-12	**Galileo Gold** D, BF	3 9-0	137^T	6-1	Hugo Palmer	won 2,000 Guineas Gp1 (1m) (1)
15 11d-11	**Gleneagles** D	3 9-0	137^T	8-15f	Aidan O'Brien (IRE)	won 2,000 Guineas Gp1 (1m) (1)
14 1-121	**Kingman** D	3 9-0	140^T	8-11f	John Gosden	won Irish 2,000 Guineas Gp1 (1m) (0)

FAVOURITES £2.92 **TRAINERS IN THIS RACE (w-pl-r)** Aidan O'Brien 3-4-20, Richard Hannon 1-2-7, Jim Bolger 1-0-2, Charlie Appleby 1-2-7, John & Thady Gosden 0-0-3, Roger Varian 0-1-2, Karl Burke 0-0-1, Andre Fabre 0-0-1
FATE OF FAVOURITES 1124132112 **POSITION OF WINNER IN MARKET** 1132153112

FOUNDED in 1839, this 2m4f handicap has come to be dominated by trainers whose main emphasis is jump racing, with Willie Mullins, Nicky Henderson, Jonjo O'Neill and David Pipe on the roll of honour since 2010.

Last year's winner

Henderson, first successful with Veiled in 2011, struck again with 7-1 shot Ahorsewithnoname, who had won a Listed mares' novice hurdle a couple of months before and had good trends-fitting Flat form from the previous season.

Form Three of the last ten winners had scored last time out but five had been unplaced.

Weight Last year's first three all came from the top six in the weights and a mark around the high 90s up to 100. Four winners and two

Key trends
▶ *Won a Flat handicap, 10/10*
▶ *Won within last five Flat starts, 9/10*
▶ *Previously ran over hurdles, 8/10*
▶ *Raced no more than once on the Flat that season, 8/10*
▶ *Officially rated 91-98, 7/10*

Other factors
▶ *Three winners were set to carry 9st 10lb (2022 winner Coltrane was ridden by a 5lb claimer)*
▶ *Only three winners had scored beyond 2m on the Flat*

runners-up have carried top weight of 9st 10lb since 2012.

Key races The Chester Cup is often informative. Last year's runner-up, Calling The Wind, had been sixth there, 2022 winner Coltrane came

off a neck second and 2021 winner Reshoun had prepped by finishing 11th there (numerous others have shown up well in both races). Five of the six Irish winners since 2012 had run recently over hurdles at the Punchestown festival. On the Flat, handicaps at Newmarket, York and Leopardstown have also been a stepping stone.

Trainers Mullins has had four winners since 2012, as well as the runner-up in 2019, 2021 and 2022. His record since 2012 is 10177011345022 0020 from 18 runners for a level-stake profit of +13pts.

Betting This is not impossibly hard, with half of the last ten winners coming from the top five in the betting. The only two successful favourites in the past 20 years were both trained by Mullins.

Story of the last ten years

FORM	WINNER	AGE & WGT	OR	SP	TRAINER	BEST RPR LAST 12 MONTHS (RUNS SINCE)
23 /115-	**Ahorsewithnoname** BF 8	9-8	96-6	7-1	Nicky Henderson	5th Cesarewitch (2m2f) (0)
22 6-422	**Coltrane** BF	5 9-5	98-3	14-1	Andrew Balding	2nd Kempton Class 2 hcap (1m4f) (4)
21 600-0	**Reshoun**	7 9-7	97-2	66-1	Ian Williams	won Newbury Class 2 hcap (2m½f) (4)
20 330-5	**Coeur De Lion**	7 8-10	91-3	16-1	Alan King	3rd Northumberland Vase (2m½f) (3)
19 101-7	**The Grand Visir**	5 9-10	100-3	12-1	Ian Williams	won Doncaster Class 3 hcap (1m6½f) (1)
18 1332-	**Lagostovegas**	6 9-3	93-3	10-1	Willie Mullins (IRE)	2nd Naas Listed (1m4f) (0)
17 1211/	**Thomas Hobson**	7 9-10	100T	4-1f	Willie Mullins (IRE)	Seasonal debut (0)
16 /21-1	**Jennies Jewel**	9 9-3	93-4	6-1	Jarlath Fahey (IRE)	won Curragh handicap (2m) (0)
15 2101-	**Clondaw Warrior**	8 9-0	89-4	5-1f	Willie Mullins (IRE)	won Leopardstown handicap (1m7f) (0)
14 120-0	**Domination**	7 9-7	92-3	12-1	Charles Byrnes (IRE)	2nd Galway handicap (2m) (2)

WINS-PL-RUNS 4yo 0-9-41, 5yo 2-12-58, 6yo+ 8-9-91 **FAVOURITES** £1.00
FATE OF FAVOURITES 5101402520 **POSITION OF WINNER IN MARKET** 7121587063

5.40 Wolferton Stakes

NAUGURATED in 2002 with the extension of Royal Ascot to a five-day meeting, this was changed in 2018 to become a 1m2f Listed conditions race for four-year-olds and up (rather than a Listed handicap).

Last year's winner Royal Champion at 16-1 became the third winner in a row at double-figure odds but fitted a number of key trends and had the adjusted Racing Post Rating in the low 120s that has been the norm since the change in 2018.

Form All six winners since 2018 had been beaten on their previous start (indeed, none had made the top three) – the most recent-last-time out scorer was Mahsoob in 2015. But all of the last six had been placed at least in a Group contest (two had won at that level).

Key races Five of the six

(Run as a handicap until 2018)

Key trends
▶ Beaten on previous start, 9/10
▶ Won on a right-handed track, 8/10
▶ Ran no more than twice that season, 8/10
▶ Won at Class 2 level or higher, 8/10
▶ Aged four or five, 8/10
▶ Drawn in single figures, 6/10 (all six drawn between five and seven)

Other factors
▶ Seven winners had finished outside the top three last time out
▶ John Gosden has won this four times since 2011, including in 2018 (Monarchs Glen) – the first time it was a conditions race rather than a handicap

winners since 2018 had run in Listed company at least on their most recent start. Two had run at Meydan over the winter; domestic 1m2f races like the Brigadier Gerard are worth checking.

Trainers Royal Champion last year was the fifth winner for a Newmarket yard in six runnings as a Listed race (the town's trainers also took six of the last nine as a handicap). Their stables are well stocked with the later-maturing, well-bred types who do well in this race.

Betting The first three winners post-2018 were in the first four in the betting; the last three have been much further down the list.

Royal Champion gets the verdict

RUN over 1m6f, this handicap for four-year-olds and upwards was introduced as part of the enhanced programme for Royal Ascot in 2020. Newmarket stables filled the first three places in the first two runnings, but North Yorkshire trainer David O'Meara struck in 2022 with 16-1 shot Get Shirty and last year Irish jumps champion Willie Mullins had the first two. Nine of the 12 runners who have finished in the first three were rated 95-101 (including every winner) and six of them had winning form over at least 1m6f.

Vauban scores last year, leading home a one-two for Willie Mullins

The ones to watch – from cool jockeys to super sires

Racing Post deputy betting editor Graeme Rodway picks out notable angles from last year's meeting

DON'T RULE OUT AN UPSET IN THE OPENER

The Queen Anne Stakes kicks off the week and it often goes one of two ways. When there is a standout horse in the line-up they usually win, but when the race lacks a star there is often an upset, and that was again the case 12 months ago when Triple Time sprang a 33-1 surprise.

Since 2010, seven of the nine favourites who went off at 11-8 or shorter won and stars like Goldikova, Frankel, Toronado, Solow, Ribchester, Palace Pier and Baaeed all got the job done. However, only one of the six favourites who went off bigger than that was successful.

In three of those six years the race went to Accidental Agent (33-1), Lord Glitters (14-1) and then Triple Time, and it's clear this is a race ripe for an upset when the market doesn't settle on a clear favourite. That looks like the case this year.

It will be fascinating to see whether Francis Graffard sends Dolayli over from France. This race went across the Channel twice from 2010 to 2015 (both trained by Freddy Head) and also was won by US-based trainer Mark Casse with Tepin in 2016. Dolayli might be this year's surprise package.

ELEMENTARY FOR WATSON IN THE SPRINTS

The best lessons are often the simplest and last year taught us Archie Watson (below) is a force to be reckoned with in the sprint races at Royal Ascot. All three of his winners in 2023 came over five and six furlongs, including two of the big ones, the King's Stand and Wokingham.

Those three winners were achieved from just seven runners in sprints across the week and, as well as Bradsell and Saint Lawrence in the aforementioned events, Watson also had Rhythm N Hooves win the Palace of Holyroodhouse and Army Ethos finish second in the Coventry.

Five of Watson's seven entries for the early-closing races at this year's meeting are in sprints, including Evade, Kylian and Action

Jamie Spencer produces a masterclass to score aboard 50-1 shot Witch Hunter in last year's Buckingham Palace Handicap

ROYAL
ASCOT
2023

Point in the Commonwealth Cup and Albasheer and Kylian in the King Charles III Stakes. All should be considered as they are huge prices.

PUT A PREMIUM ON PATIENCE IN THE SADDLE

It has long been widely known that the straight track at Ascot tends to suit horses who are ridden patiently and nobody is better at employing such tactics than Jamie Spencer. Anyone who was in any doubt about whether Spencer still had it was given a big reminder last year.

Spencer produced a big contender for ride of the week when landing the Buckingham Palace on 50-1 outsider Witch Hunter and then probably bettered it to take the Queen Elizabeth II Jubilee aboard 80-1 shot Khaadem. It's hard to believe that either horse would have won without Spencer's assistance.

He might not be everyone's favourite, but the Ascot straight course is his playground and don't

23

forget that. It looks like the certainty of the week that he will hit the frame on a big-priced runner at some point and it will probably only take one to win for a profit.

The other two riders who impressed were Neil Callan and Rossa Ryan. Callan, who has returned from Hong Kong in recent years, partnered Triple Time and Burdett Road to big-priced wins, and Ryan was responsible for 150-1 Valiant Force and 22-1 scorer Jimi Hendrix.

Jockeyship is as important as ever at Royal Ascot and apart from Ryan Moore, who the market is all over, there weren't many better than Spencer, Callan and Ryan 12 months ago.

IT'S NOT ALWAYS THE BIG NAMES WHO GET THE HEADLINES

With the Cheltenham Festival so heavily dominated by Willie Mullins it's easy to fall into the trap of thinking that Royal Ascot is also controlled by the superpowers, but that isn't the case.

The eight Group 1s at last season's meeting went to seven different trainers and among the winners were Julie Camacho, Charlie Hills,

Kevin Ryan and Archie Watson. Aidan O'Brien won only one and John and Thady Gosden two, so it's quite plausible that the smaller yards can compete.

Only one favourite and one second favourite were successful at the top table and four of the eight Group 1 winners were double-figure prices, so Royal Ascot is gloriously competitive.

STICK WITH THE SUPER SIX SIRES

While one trainer might not be dominant, a set of super sires came to the fore last year and 14 of the 35 races (40 per cent) went to the offspring of just five stallions – Galileo (four), Frankel (three), Siyouni (three), Kingman (two) and Wootton Bassett (two).

When you add in Dubawi, who had five winners in 2022 but an uncharacteristically low total of just one last year, you're left with six super sires who hold the key to Royal Ascot success.

Fastnet Rock might not have sired a winner himself, but three winners came from dams he had sired and two were bred along a Galileo cross in Okita Soushi and Warm Heart. They both won over 1m4f, so Galileo x Fastnet Rock mare is worth looking out for at the trip.

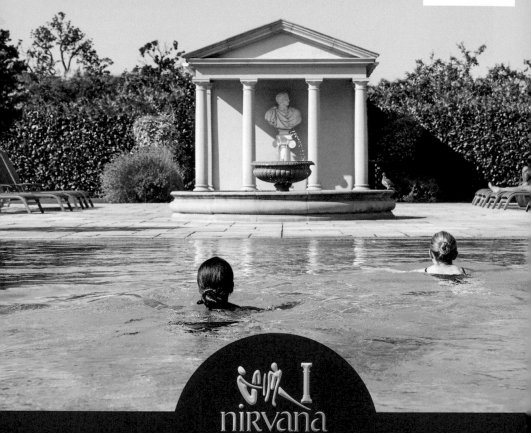

Escape to relaxation

Unwind in our Spa Garden

Evening tranquillity

Our serene Spa awaits

DAY TWO

The Group 1 Prince of Wales's Stakes is the glittering centrepiece of day two but elsewhere there has been shuffling of the card, including course changes for the Duke of Cambridge Stakes and the Kensington Palace Handicap.

Run over a mile and a quarter for four-year-olds and upwards, the Prince of Wales's regularly features among the most important and influential races of the season and last year was no exception.

Mostahdaf was a somewhat surprising winner at 10-1 in a select field of six but there was no fluke about his decisive four-length margin of victory and he went on to underline his quality with another Group 1 triumph in the International at York.

He was rated 128 in the end-of-year World's Best Racehorse Rankings, making him joint-second on the planet and the best in Britain.

Since being revived in its current format in 1968, the Prince of Wales's has had a Classic quality for older horses and a strong international flavour. There have been eight wins for Ireland and five for France in a race that showcases the cream of European talent.

The day's course changes take the Kensington Palace to the straight mile in response to feedback from participants about congestion in a 20-runner handicap on the round course, while the Duke of Cambridge moves the opposite way (to the round mile from the straight) to maintain the balance in round/straight races.

The Kensington Palace also moves back down the order to race six, with the Queen's Vase swapping to slot back in as race two.

The card opens with the Queen Mary Stakes, the meeting's premier race for two-year-old fillies and one of three Group 2 events on the card.

The emphasis switches from speedsters to stayers in the Queen's Vase, the day's longest race over a mile and three-quarters. This Group 2 contest for three-year-olds is often a proving ground for potential St Leger contenders.

The third Group 2 race on the card is the Duke of Cambridge for fillies and mares aged four and upwards.

The big betting race is the Royal Hunt Cup, the first of the week's heritage handicaps. A maximum field of 30 runners will charge down the straight mile in this hotly competitive battle for three-year-olds and upwards.

That is followed by the Kensington Palace, a handicap for fillies and mares aged four and upwards, and the day finishes with the Listed Windsor Castle Stakes. The finale gives the fast and early two-year-olds another turn over five furlongs, although unlike the Queen Mary it is open to both sexes.

Last year's winners of the two Wednesday juvenile contests ended up meeting in the Grade 1 Breeders' Cup Juvenile Turf Sprint at Santa Anita in November and victory went to Windsor Castle winner Big Evs with Crimson Advocate (the Queen Mary scorer) back in sixth.

Wednesday June 19

RUNNING ORDER

2.30 **Queen Mary Stakes** (Group 2) Last year's winner: Crimson Advocate 9-1	**5f** 2yo fillies	£150,000
3.05 **Queen's Vase** (Group 2) Last year's winner: Gregory Evensf	**1m6f** 3yo	£265,000
3.45 **Duke of Cambridge Stakes** (Group 2) Last year's winner: Rogue Millennium 10-1	**1m** 4yo+ fillies and mares	£225,000
4.25 **Prince of Wales's Stakes** (Group 1) Last year's winner: Mostahdaf 10-1	**1m2f** 4yo+	£1,000,000
5.05 **Royal Hunt Cup** (Heritage Handicap) Last year's winner: Jimi Hendrix 22-1	**1m** 3yo+	£175,000
5.40 **Kensington Palace Stakes** (Handicap) Last year's winner: Villanova Queen 25-1	**1m** 4yo+ fillies and mares	£110,000
6.15 **Windsor Castle Stakes** (Listed) Last year's winner: Big Evs 20-1	**5f** 2yo	£110,000

Race value is total prize-money

2.30 Queen Mary Stakes

FOUNDED in honour of the consort of King George V and first run in 1921, this five-furlong dash is the premier race at the meeting restricted to two-year-old fillies.

Last year's winner

Crimson Advocate became the fifth US-trained winner of this race since 2009 – with George Weaver joining pioneer Wesley Ward on the roll of honour – and the 9-1 shot fitted every key trend. She had won one of the two US automatic qualifiers for Royal Ascot held at Gulfstream Park for the first time last May.

Form High-class winning form is virtually essential and 12 of the 15 winners since 2009 had scored last time out.

Key races The Marygate

Stakes at York is the main northern stepping stone, with Ceiling Kitty (2012) and Signora Cabello (2018) the most recent to double

Key trends

▶ *By a sire with stamina index between 5.9f and 8.4f, ten winners in last ten runnings*
▶ *Top-three finish last time out, 10/10 (eight won)*
▶ *Adjusted Racing Post Rating of at least 103, 9/10*
▶ *Rated within 9lb of RPR top-rated, 8/10*
▶ *Distance winner, 6/10*

Other factors

▶ *Two of the four not to have won over the trip were trained by Wesley Ward – one had won over 4½f, while the other was still a maiden*

up. Ward likes to prep his juveniles at Keeneland, although the Gulfstream qualifiers are likely to become important now. Bath novices can be worth noting.

Trainers Ward has had four of the 15 winners since he started to target Royal Ascot in 2009. Other trainers noted for fast horses also appear on the roll of honour, including Richard Hannon snr, Mick Channon, Eddie Lynam and Clive Cox (along with Ward, they account for nearly 40 per cent of the winners in the last 30 years).

Betting Nine of the last 15 winners were in the top three in the betting and it is worth noting that three of the longer-priced winners came from northern stables (even though two of them had high-class winning form in the Marygate at York).

Story of the last ten years

	FORM	WINNER		AGE & WGT	Adj RPR	SP	TRAINER	BEST RPR LAST 12 MONTHS (RUNS SINCE)
23	31	**Crimson Advocate**	D	2 9-2	104-2	9-1	George Weaver (USA)	won Gulfstream qualifier (5f) (0)
22	1	**Dramatised**	D	2 9-2	113T	5-2f	Karl Burke	won Newmarket Class 3 maiden (5f) (0)
21	212	**Quick Suzy**		2 9-0	108-2	8-1	Gavin Cromwell (IRE)	2nd Naas Gp3 (6f) (0)
20	1	**Campanelle**	D	2 9-0	104-3	9-2	Wesley Ward (USA)	won Gulfstream maiden (5f) (0)
19	21	**Raffle Prize**		2 9-0	103-12	18-1	Mark Johnston	won Chester Class 2 maiden (6f) (0)
18	411	**Signora Cabella**	D	2 9-0	105-7	25-1	John Quinn	won York Listed (5f) (0)
17	1	**Heartache**	D	2 9-0	107-3	5-1	Clive Cox	won Bath Class 4 novice (5f) (0)
16	1	**Lady Aurelia**		2 9-0	112T	2-1f	Wesley Ward (USA)	won Keeneland maiden (4½f) (0)
15	3	**Acapulco**	BF	2 9-0	91-15	5-2f	Wesley Ward (USA)	3rd Churchill Downs maiden (4½f) (0)
14	61	**Anthem Alexander**	D	2 9-0	106-9	9-4f	Eddie Lynam (IRE)	won Tipperary maiden (5f) (0)

FAVOURITES £3.25

TRAINERS IN THIS RACE (w-pl-r) Wesley Ward 3-3-13, Karl Burke 1-1-7, Clive Cox 1-1-8, Richard Hannon 0-2-11, Aidan O'Brien 0-1-7, Jessica Harrington 0-0-2, William Haggas 0-3-4, Andrew Balding 0-0-2, Richard Fahey 0-0-11

FATE OF FAVOURITES 1112030213 **POSITION OF WINNER IN MARKET** 1112902214

ATING back to 1838 and run under its current name since 1960, this 1m6f race is restricted to three-year-olds and designed to bring along future St Leger and Cup horses over staying trips. This is the eighth year since a reduction in distance from two miles.

Last year's winner

Gregory emphatically fitted every trend and the even-money favourite made his 6lb advantage on Racing Post Ratings count.

Form Winning form is not essential, given that some will come here after being tried on the Classics route, although the last four winners had scored last time.

Key races Aidan O'Brien is likely to send one or more of his lesser lights from the Classics trail, while British

---

(Run over 2m until 2017)

Key trends

▸ *Top-three finish last time out, 9/10*
▸ *By a sire with a stamina index of 1m2f+, 8/10*
▸ *Adjusted RPR of at least 108, 8/10*
▸ *Won within last two starts, 7/10*
▸ *Rated within 8lb of RPR top-rated, 7/10*

Other factors

▸ *The only trainers to have won since 2000 are Sir Michael Stoute (three), Saeed bin Suroor (two), Mark Johnston (seven), Aidan O'Brien (seven), John Gosden (twice), Andrew Balding, Charlie Appleby and Roger Varian (all once)*
▸ *Five winners ran in a Listed or Group race last time out*

---

successes tend to come from a more low-key route through maidens and even handicaps. Gregory won the Listed Cocked Hat Stakes at Goodwood, a minor Classic trial, but the three scorers before him were maiden winners who had missed the trials.

Trainers The race has been monopolised by stables with the best resources for staying and middle-distance horses (see panel left).

Betting The market is often a good guide to the best prospects from the big stables, with 13 of the last 16 winners coming from the top two in the betting. In that period, backing runners from the dominant stables that made the top two in the betting would have yielded a level-stakes profit of +18.36pts.

Story of the last ten years

	FORM	WINNER	AGE & WGT	Adj RPR	SP	TRAINER	BEST RPR LAST 12 MONTHS (RUNS SINCE)
23	11	**Gregory**	3 9-2	123^T	Evsf	John & Thady Gosden	won Goodwood Listed (1m3f) (0)
22	1-1	**Eldar Eldarov**	3 9-2	111^{-8}	5-2f	Roger Varian	won Newcastle Class 5 novice (1m2f) (0)
21	21	**Kemari**	3 9-0	108^{-12}	15-2	Charlie Appleby	won Yarmouth Class 4 mdn (1m3½f) (0)
20	221-	**Santiago**	3 9-0	102^{-18}	10-3	Aidan O'Brien (IRE)	2nd Galway maiden auction (7f) (1)
19	28-23	**Dashing Willoughby**	3 9-0	118^{-8}	6-1	Andrew Balding	2nd Newbury Class 3 cond (1m2f) (1)
18	1-329	**Kew Gardens**	3 9-0	121^{-7}	10-3	Aidan O'Brien (IRE)	won Newmarket Listed (1m2f) (3)
17	41-12	**Stradivarius** BF	3 9-0	114^{-3}	11-2	John Gosden	2nd Chester Class 3 hcap (1m4½f) (0)
16	3-213	**Sword Fighter**	3 9-3	99^{-16}	33-1	Aidan O'Brien (IRE)	3rd Naas conditions (1m4f) (0)
15	212-	**Aloft**	3 9-3	123^T	5-2f	Aidan O'Brien (IRE)	2nd Racing Post Trophy Gp1 (1m) (0)
14	13-52	**Hartnell**	3 9-3	115^T	7-2	Mark Johnston	2nd Lingfield Derby Trial (1m3½f) (0)

FAVOURITES -£1.00

TRAINERS IN THIS RACE (w-pl-r) Aidan O'Brien 4-5-21, Roger Varian 1-0-1, Andrew Balding 1-3-11, Charlie Appleby 1-3-9, John & Thady Gosden 1-1-6, Sir Michael Stoute 0-0-2, William Haggas 0-0-4

FATE OF FAVOURITES 3144004211 **POSITION OF WINNER IN MARKET** 2102223211

THIS Group 2 contest for older fillies and mares has been run over the straight mile but switches to the round mile this year, which will change the influence of the draw. The race was introduced in 2004 with the aim of encouraging connections to keep female runners in training beyond their three-year-old campaigns.

Last year's winner Rogue Millennium gave Newmarket trainer Tom Clover his first Royal Ascot success with a neck victory at 10-1. Interestingly, it was her first run at a mile (having always raced at 1m2f-1m4f) but she had the requisite class on form and ratings.

Form High-class form is important, with the majority of winners having scored already at Group level, although Rogue Millennium (a Listed winner) became the fourth in five years not to have done that. Saffron

Key trends

▶ *Distance winner, 8/10*
▶ *Rated within 6lb of RPR top-rated, 8/10*
▶ *Top-three finish that season, 7/10 (one exception making reappearance)*
▶ *Adjusted RPR of at least 121, 8/10*
▶ *Had won a Group race, 6/10*

Other factors

▶ *Winners of the Dahlia at Newmarket finished 9412*
▶ *Two winners had run at the previous year's meeting – one in the Coronation Stakes (1) and one in this race (2)*

Beach in 2022 was the first to defy a Group 1 penalty, being the 17th to try and having ended the previous season with victory in the Group 1 Sun Chariot Stakes. Qemah in 2017 was another previous Group 1 winner.

Key races The Snowdrop Fillies' Stakes and Magnolia Stakes at Kempton have been used as a stepping stone from all-weather to turf in recent years. Turf races to note are the Dahlia Stakes at Newmarket and the previous year's Atalanta Stakes at Sandown.

Trainers John Gosden (latterly in partnership with son Thady) and Sir Michael Stoute have each had four winners.

Betting There have been six successful favourites (including joint) in the 20 runnings.

Story of the last ten years

	FORM	WINNER		AGE & WGT	Adj RPR	SP	TRAINER	BEST RPR LAST 12 MONTHS (RUNS SINCE)
23	0-232	**Rogue Millennium**		4 9-2	124-4	10-1	Tom Clover	2nd Middleton Stakes Gp2 (1m2½f) (0)
22	011-4	**Saffron Beach**	D	4 9-7	125-3	5-2j	Jane Chapple-Hyam	won Sun Chariot Stakes Gp1 (1m) (1)
21	71-54	**Indie Angel**	D	4 9-0	119-11	22-1	John & Thady Gosden	won Lingfield Listed (1m) (2)
20	111-1	**Nazeef**	D	4 9-0	121-4	10-3	John Gosden	won Newmarket Class 3 hcap (1m) (1)
19	1222-	**Move Swiftly**	D, BF	4 9-0	122-6	9-1	William Haggas	2nd Newmarket Class 2 hcap (1m) (1)
18	197-3	**Aljazzi**	D	5 9-0	128T	9-2	Marco Botti	won Atalanta Stakes Gp3 (1m) (3)
17	113-2	**Qemah**	C, D	4 9-0	131T	5-2f	Jean-Claude Rouget (FR)	won Prix Rothschild Gp1 (1m) (2)
16	7-111	**Usherette**	D	4 9-3	128-1	9-4f	Andre Fabre (FR)	won Dahlia Stakes Gp2 (1m1f) (0)
15	00-33	**Amazing Maria**		4 9-0	119-9	25-1	David O'Meara	3rd Lanwades Stud Stakes Gp2 (1m) (0)
14	712-2	**Integral**	D, BF	4 9-0	130T	9-4f	Sir Michael Stoute	2nd Sun Chariot Stakes Gp1 (1m) (1)

WINS-PL-RUNS 4yo 9-10-88, 5yo 1-8-21, 6yo+ 0-0-6 **FAVOURITES** £1.56

TRAINERS IN THIS RACE (w-pl-r) David O'Meara 1-2-5, John & Thady Gosden 1-0-1, William Haggas 1-0-4, Francis Graffard 0-0-1, Charlie Appleby 0-0-2, Roger Varian 0-0-7, Joseph O'Brien 0-0-3, Hugo Palmer 0-0-1, Ralph Beckett 0-1-2

FATE OF FAVOURITES 1511033313 **POSITION OF WINNER IN MARKET** 1511263815

SASSI HOLFORD

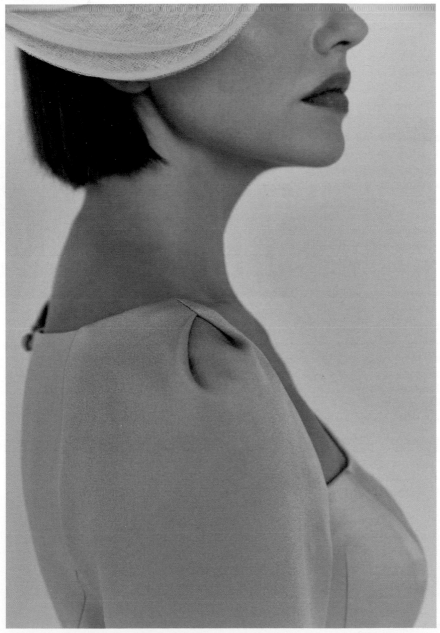

Hat by Jane Taylor

MADE IN ENGLAND

278 Brompton Road, London, SW3 2AB

020 4576 2506 • sassiholford.com

FIRST run in 1862 and reduced in distance to a mile and a quarter in 1968, this Group 1 showpiece is often the top-ranked contest of Royal Ascot, based on the ratings of the first four finishers.

Last year's winner

Mostahdaf was one of the lowest-rated in a strong six-runner line-up but was within the right range and fitted every key trend. The biggest question mark was whether he could step up to Group 1 success for the first time but the 10-1 shot answered that in emphatic style with a four-length win.

Form The typical winner has already proved top class, both in terms of races won and ratings achieved, and Mostahdaf was only the seventh winner in the 24 runnings since the race was promoted to elite status in 2000 who was scoring at Group 1 level for the first time. It is interesting that all seven have struck in the last 14 editions, although it is equally worth noting that most of those had strong Group 1 placings on their record already.

Key races Since 2000 Poet's Word, Crystal Ocean and Lord North are the only ones of the 21 winners who had already raced that season not to have posted their most

Story of the last ten years

	FORM	WINNER	AGE & WGT	Adj RPR	SP	TRAINER	BEST RPR LAST 12 MONTHS (RUNS SINCE)
23	10-14	**Mostahdaf** D	5 9-2	134-5	10-1	John & Thady Gosden	won Riyadh Gp2 (1m2½f) (1)
22	11-13	**State Of Rest** D, BF	4 9-2	133-5	5-1	Joseph O'Brien (IRE)	won Cox Plate Gp1 (1m2f) (2)
21	/111-	**Love**	4 8-11	141T	11-10f	Aidan O'Brien (IRE)	won Yorkshire Oaks Gp1 (1m4f) (0)
20	121-1	**Lord North** D	4 9-0	135-4	5-1	John Gosden	won Brigadier Gerard Stakes Gp3 (1m2f) (0)
19	22-11	**Crystal Ocean** C, D	5 9-0	141T	3-1	Sir Michael Stoute	2nd King George Gp1 (1m4f) (4)
18	26-21	**Poet's Word** D	5 9-0	134-11	11-2	Sir Michael Stoute	2nd Irish Champion Stakes Gp1 (1m2f) (4)
17	12-71	**Highland Reel** C, D	5 9-0	138-1	9-4	Aidan O'Brien (IRE)	2nd Prix de l'Arc de Triomphe Gp1 (1m4f) (4)
16	11-15	**My Dream Boat** D	4 9-0	134-11	16-1	Clive Cox	won Gordon Richards Stakes Gp3 (1m2f) (1)
15	2/13-	**Free Eagle** D	4 9-0	136-4	5-2f	Dermot Weld (IRE)	3rd Champion Stakes Gp1 (1m2f) (0)
14	122-0	**The Fugue** D	5 8-11	140-8	11-2	John Gosden	won Irish Champion Stakes Gp1 (1m2f) (3)

WINS-PL-RUNS 4yo 5-10-36, 5yo 5-3-24, 6yo+ 0-1-10 **FAVOURITES** -£4.40

TRAINERS IN THIS RACE (w-pl-r) Aidan O'Brien 2-4-11, Sir Michael Stoute 2-2-9, John & Thady Gosden 1-0-2, Joseph O'Brien 1-0-1, Roger Varian 0-0-2, Jerome Reynier 0-0-1, William Haggas 0-1-5

FATE OF FAVOURITES 3168224122 **POSITION OF WINNER IN MARKET** 2162223135

4.25 Prince of Wales's Stakes

Mostahdaf beats a high-class field by four lengths last year

Other factors
▶Twelve fillies have gone to post, finishing 135242566213
▶Since Rakti in 2004, two winners landed the prize on their reappearance (Free Eagle in 2015 and Love in 2021)
▶Four winners had previously landed a Group 1

Roll of honour
Longest-priced winner
Bob Back 33-1 (1985)

Shortest-priced winner
Royal Palace 1-4 (1968)

Most successful trainer
5 wins: **Sir Henry Cecil**
Lucky Wednesday (1977), Gunner B (1978), Perpendicular (1992), Placerville (1993), Bosra Sham (1997); **John Gosden** Muhtarram (1994, 1995), The Fugue (2014), Lord North (2020), Mostahdaf (2023, joint with Thady Gosden)

Most successful jockey
5 wins: **Pat Eddery**
Record Run (1975), English Spring (1986), Two Timing (1989), Batshoof (1990), Placerville (1993)

Most successful owner
5 wins: **Godolphin**
Faithful Son (1998), Dubai Millennium (2000), Fantastic Light (2001), Grandera (2002), Rewilding (2011)

*All figures since 1968

recent outing at Group 1 level, although a trial to note at a lower level is the Group 3 Gordon Richards Stakes at Sandown (won by Al Kazeem in 2013, My Dream Boat in 2016 and Crystal Ocean in 2019). Another significant Group 3 is the Brigadier Gerard Stakes, also at Sandown, which was won by Poet's Word in 2018 after his earlier good run in Group 1 company when second in the Sheema Classic and by Lord North in 2020 (when it was run at Haydock).

Horses coming off a break after a good performance on Dubai World Cup night also have a decent record, with Mostahdaf (fourth in the Sheema Classic) the most recent of five such winners this century.

The Tattersalls Gold Cup has been the chosen warm-up for six winners during that period (among that number only Azamour in 2005 and State Of Rest in 2022 were beaten at the Curragh), while France's two early-season Group 1s, the Prix d'Ispahan and the Prix Ganay, have been a launch pad for four winners between them.

Trainers Mostahdaf put John Gosden (four wins on his own and one with son Thady) level with Sir Henry Cecil on five, the modern-day record. Aidan O'Brien, Sir Michael Stoute and Saeed bin Suroor are all on four.

Betting In a sign that the cream rises to the top, only three of the 24 winners since 2000 were outside the top three in the betting.

FIRST run in 1843, this is the first of the week's heritage handicaps down the straight course, with 30 runners fanning out in the mile contest for three-year-olds and up.

Last year's winner Jimi Hendrix struck at 22-1 for Ralph Beckett, although he scored well on trends with winning form at the trip and in a sizeable field. He was in the right place on official ratings too.

Form Most recent winners arrived off the back of a top-four finish, though rarely after a victory, and had some big-field experience.

Draw Jimi Hendrix (stall seven) was only the third of the last ten winners with a single-figure draw, coming home two lengths in front from a far-side group of 14. However, with the majority of recent winners coming from the highest ten stalls, the near side is often the place to be (the next six after Jimi Hendrix were drawn in the 20s).

Key races The Lincoln, Spring Cup (won by Jimi Hendrix last year) and Victoria Cup provide a road map, but perhaps most notably seven of the last ten winners had run in one of the Cambridgeshires at Newmarket or the Curragh the previous year.

Betting The market has been no better than a fair guide, with eight of the 14 winners outside the top seven in the betting since Forgotten Voice was the last winning favourite in 2009.

Key trends
- *Aged four or five, 9/10 (eight aged four)*
- *Carried between 9st and 9st 5lb, 9/10*
- *Officially rated between 96 and 103, 8/10*
- *Won or placed in a field of at least 13 runners, 8/10*
- *Top-three finish at least once that season, 8/10 (both exceptions making reappearance)*
- *Ran between one and three times that campaign, 7/10*
- *Distance winner, 6/10*

Other factors
- *There have been only three winning favourites in the last 35 years – True Panache in 1989, Yeast in 1996 and Forgotten Voice in 2009*
- *Only three of the last ten winners were drawn in single figures, while 2022 winner Dark Shift was the only one drawn between stalls 12 and 20*
- *Four winners wore some form of headgear*

Story of the last ten years

	FORM	WINNER		AGE & WGT	OR	SP	TRAINER	BEST RPR LAST 12 MONTHS (RUNS SINCE)
23	5-018	**Jimi Hendrix** D, BF		4 9-5	103-8	22-1	Ralph Beckett	won Newbury Class 2 hcap (1m) (1)
22	11-01	**Dark Shift** (5ex) CD		4 9-1	96-1	13-2	Charlie Hills	won Nottingham Class 2 hcap (1m1½f) (0)
21	2-334	**Real World**		4 8-6	94-6	18-1	Saeed bin Suroor	3rd Meydan Listed hcap (1m2f) (1)
20	630-2	**Dark Vision** BF		4 9-1	100T	15-2	Mark Johnston	2nd Newcastle Class 2 handicap (1m) (0)
19	4630-	**Afaak** D		5 9-3	103-3	20-1	Charlie Hills	2nd Royal Hunt Cup (1m) (4)
18	11-14	**Settle For Bay** D		4 9-1	99-8	16-1	David Marnane (IRE)	4th Leopardstown handicap (7f) (0)
17	-4803	**Zhui Feng**		4 9-0	100-3	25-1	Amanda Perrett	4th Winter Derby Gp3 (1m2f) (3)
16	125-1	**Portage** (5ex) CD		4 9-5	105-7	10-1	Mick Halford (IRE)	5th Newmarket Class 2 hcap (1m1f) (1)
15	43-02	**Gm Hopkins** D, BF		4 9-3	103-2	8-1	John Gosden	2nd Newbury Class 2 handicap (1m) (0)
14	5950-	**Field Of Dream** C		7 9-1	101-1	20-1	Jamie Osborne	won Newmarket Class 2 hcap (7f) (4)

WINS-PL-RUNS 4yo 8-18-127, 5yo 1-6-68, 6yo+ 1-6-90 **FAVOURITES** -£10.00

FATE OF FAVOURITES 0000050200 **POSITION OF WINNER IN MARKET** 8230903920

NOW in its fourth year, this mile handicap for older fillies and mares rated 0-105 has proved a tricky test for punters. There is a new puzzle this year as the race switches from the round to the straight course, although potentially there will be fewer hard-luck stories with the runners more spread out. Dave Loughnane had the first two (Lola Showgirl at 12-1 and Ffion at 10-1) in the inaugural running and both had got in at the bottom end of the weights off ratings of 81; in 2022 the first three were Marco Botti's Rising Star (40-1), Random Harvest (40-1) and Isola Rossa (22-1); and last year the first two were Villanova Queen (25-1) for Jessica Harrington and Don't Tell Claire (22-1).

Villanova Queen and Colin Keane after last year's win

ESTABLISHED in 1839, this five-furlong dash for two-year-olds is open to colts, geldings and fillies.

Last year's winner Big Evs, having been runner-up in a Redcar novice on his only start, bucked several key trends to strike at 20-1 for Mick Appleby, although he proved top class by the end of the season with victory in the Grade 1 Breeders' Cup Juvenile Turf Sprint (along with the Group 2 Flying Childers and Group 3 Molecomb).

Form Most winners had a decent level of form, with five of the last ten having been tried in Listed company, although three of the last five went against the established trend in not having lost their maiden tag before coming here.

Key trends
▶ *No more than three runs, 10/10*
▶ *By a sire with a stamina index of 6.5f-8.1f, 9/10*
▶ *Beaten last time out, 7/10 (two finished outside top three)*
▶ *Distance winner, 6/10 (three exceptions were maidens)*
▶ *Double-figure draw, 6/10*

Other factors
▶ *Fillies won five in a row from 1996 to 2000 but only one has placed in the last ten years*
▶ *The 2022 winner Little Big Bear was RPR top-rated, but six of the other nine were between 7lb and 19lb off top*

Key races The high-level route involves a Listed contest (five of the last ten winners had run in the National at Sandown, the Marble Hill at the Curragh or in a US Listed); the other path is through maidens and novices.

Trainers It is notable that 11 current trainers achieved their first Royal Ascot success in this contest, most recently Appleby last year. Perhaps the less high-profile stables save their best hopes for this contest, knowing that the big guns will aim their main fire at the more important juvenile races.

Betting This has proved the juvenile race most open to a surprise result in recent years, with ten of the last 18 winners 12-1 or bigger. Even the major stables can produce a long-odds winner and just five of the last ten winners came from the top six in the betting.

Story of the last ten years

	FORM	WINNER	AGE & WGT	Adj RPR	SP	TRAINER	BEST RPR LAST 12 MONTHS (RUNS SINCE)
23	2	**Big Evs**	2 9-3	88-19	20-1	Mick Appleby	2nd Redcar Class 4 novice (0)
22	21	**Little Big Bear** D	2 9-5	115T	6-5f	Aidan O'Brien (IRE)	won Naas maiden (5f) (0)
21	116	**Chipotle** CD	2 9-3	99-7	22-1	Eve Johnson Houghton	won Ascot Class 2 condtions (5f) (1)
20	3	**Tactical**	2 9-3	95-3	7-2f	Andrew Balding	3rd Newmarket Class 5 novice (5f) (0)
19	52	**Southern Hills**	2 9-3	105-4	7-1	Aidan O'Brien (IRE)	2nd Navan maiden (5f) (0)
18	21	**Soldier's Call** D	2 9-3	97-14	12-1	Archie Watson	won Haydock Class 4 novice (5f) (0)
17	14	**Sound And Silence** D	2 9-3	101-11	16-1	Charlie Appleby	4th Sandown Listed (5f) (0)
16	1	**Ardad** D	2 9-3	94-14	20-1	John Gosden	won Yarmouth Class 4 novice (5f) (0)
15	212	**Washington DC** D, BF	2 9-3	106-2	5-1	Aidan O'Brien (IRE)	2nd Curragh Listed (5f) (0)
14	13	**Hootenanny** BF	2 9-3	95-13	7-2f	Wesley Ward (USA)	3rd Pimlico Listed (5f) (0)

FAVOURITES £1.20

TRAINERS IN THIS RACE (w-pl-r) Aidan O'Brien 3-2-13, Wesley Ward 1-0-13, Andrew Balding 1-0-5, Charlie Appleby 1-1-3, Archie Watson 1-1-14, Eve Johnson Houghton 1-0-4, Kevin Ryan 0-2-3, David O'Meara 0-1-8, Richard Fahey 0-1-9, William Haggas 0-2-3, Roger Varian 0-0-4, Clive Cox, 0-0-3, Richard Hannon 0-0-13

FATE OF FAVOURITES 1300041712 **POSITION OF WINNER IN MARKET** 1207731018

EXPERT VIEW

Racing Post tipsters pick their early fancies

COWARDOFTHECOUNTY
Coventry Stakes

I was on duty at the Curragh the day Cowardofthecounty won his maiden and he dwarfed most of his rivals in the parade ring. He's a smashing specimen who seems to have all the right things in all the right places and he showed plenty of raw ability to gun down the smart and streetwise Whistlejacket, who traded at an in-running low of 1.03 on the Betfair Exchange.

It looked all over bar the shouting two furlongs out as Whistlejacket skipped clear, but Cowardofthecounty picked up really well to score going away by two and a half lengths. There was a yawning gap back to the third.

The runner-up bolted up afterwards, posting an RPR of 101, and Cowardofthecounty is unquestionably the best juvenile I've seen this season.
David Jennings

ELMALKA
Coronation Stakes

Despite showing signs of inexperience in the 1,000 Guineas, Elmalka managed to pull the race out of the fire, which highlights the ability she has.

She had to pass everything to get her head in front and, although she had only a neck to spare over Porta Fortuna at the line, her performance can be marked up considerably.

A longer trip will suit her in time, but she should confirm the Guineas form if she's given the green light for the Coronation.
Nick Watts

HENRY LONGFELLOW
St James's Palace Stakes

Just about everything that could have gone wrong did go wrong for Henry Longfellow in the French 2,000 Guineas, where he surrendered his unbeaten record. Ryan Moore would love another go at the ride, you would imagine.

That said, it was Henry Longfellow's first start of the year and there's a long season ahead, so all is not lost.

I began the season thinking this would turn out to be Ballydoyle's best three-year-old and I'm not giving up on that theory yet. He could still be the 2024 Paddington.
David Jennings

JASOUR
Commonwealth Cup

Jasour looked really good when winning the Group 2 July Stakes as a two-year-old but became hard to settle and lost his way afterwards.

However, he looked better than ever on trials day at Ascot, scything through the field and looking for all the world like a Commonwealth Cup winner.

Clearly he relishes the course and distance and, granted fast ground, he'll give Vandeek and the rest plenty to think about.
Tom Segal

MAKE HASTE
Queen Mary Stakes

Diego Dias is a trainer going places and Make Haste could take him to those places, starting in the Queen Mary.

This Blue Point filly burst clear in the closing stages of a hot-looking sprint maiden at Naas on her debut and was obviously expected to do so given she went off at 16-5.

She's a 75,000gns yearling by an exciting

young sire and looks to have inherited plenty of his pace. The Queen Mary seems the plan and she ought to take a bit of pegging back in that.
David Jennings

PASSENGER
Prince of Wales's Stakes

Sir Michael Stoute's abilities with older horses are well known and he could have great fun with Passenger this year.

Aside from one blip in last year's Derby, the four-year-old has shown progressive form and easily got the better of Israr in the Group 2 Huxley Stakes at Chester on his return from a 258-day break.

With only five starts, you would have to think the best is yet to come and he's ready for a step back into Group 1 company.
Nick Watts

PORTA FORTUNA
Coronation Stakes

This year's 1,000 Guineas might not have been the strongest given that the first five finished in a heap.

However, runner-up Porta Fortuna was the only filly in the frame who hadn't had a prep run and she might well be the one who takes the biggest step forward.

She won at the royal meeting last year and, on decent ground, might well put herself at the head of her miling division.
Tom Segal

ROHAAN
Wokingham Handicap

Winner of the Wokingham in 2021 and 2022 off marks of 112 and 109, Rohaan could get into his favourite race off 102 this time.

On 2,000 Guineas day he shaped nicely at Newmarket

– a track he doesn't like – when fifth of 15 behind Desert Cop and his 6f Ascot form figures outside of Group 1 company are 11111.

The six-year-old sprinter should be at his peak now and makes considerable punting appeal.
Richard Birch

ROSALLION
St James's Palace Stakes

Rosallion is held in the highest regard by Richard Hannon and shaped like the best horse in the 2,000 Guineas at Newmarket. He powered through the race on the bridle and was matched at evens in running, but couldn't stay with winner Notable Speech in the final furlong.

Rosallion was making his seasonal return following a 216-day absence, whereas Notable Speech was fit from the all-weather, and maybe that proved the difference.

There should be plenty more to come from Rosallion with that run under his belt and the Hannon team won the St James's Palace with Canford Cliffs (2010) and Barney Roy (2017), who both improved on placed efforts in the first Classic.
Graeme Rodway

Jasour: big contender for the Commonwealth Cup

DAY THREE

RUNNING ORDER

2.30 **Norfolk Stakes** (Group 2) Last year's winner: Valiant Force 150-1	**5f** 2yo	£150,000
3.05 **King George V Stakes** (Handicap) Last year's winner: Desert Hero 18-1	**1m4f** 3yo	£110,000
3.45 **Ribblesdale Stakes** (Group 2) Last year's winner: Warm Heart 13-2	**1m4f** 3yo fillies	£250,000
4.25 **Gold Cup** (Group 1) Last year's winner: Courage Mon Ami 15-2	**2m4f** 4yo+	£650,000
5.05 **Britannia Stakes** (Heritage Handicap) Last year's winner: Docklands 6-1f	**1m** 3yo colts & geldings	£120,000
5.40 **Hampton Court Stakes** (Group 3) Last year's winner: Waipiro 7-1	**1m2f** 3yo	£150,000
6.15 **Buckingham Palace Stakes** (Handicap) Last year's winner: Witch Hunter 50-1	**7f** 3yo+	£110,000

Race value is total prize-money

Thursday June 20

Gold Cup day is draped in tradition at the heart of the five-day meeting and is largely untouched by change, apart from this year's slight adjustments to start times from the third race onwards.

Also known as Ladies' Day, the occasion is an important date both in the racing calendar and the social season.

Established in 1807, the Gold Cup is the meeting's oldest race and one of the longest at two and a half miles. Having enjoyed a resurgence in popularity in recent years, the Group 1 contest is the staying highlight of the racing year.

Every other race on the card is at least a mile shorter, with a strong focus on three-year-old talent.

The mile-and-a-half contests are the King George V Stakes, a handicap for three-year-olds that is usually won by a lightly raced improver from a powerful stable, and the Group 2 Ribblesdale Stakes. This is the meeting's middle-distance feature for three-year-old fillies and often attracts graduates from the Oaks at Epsom or at least one of the trials.

Those two races produced notable winners last year. Desert Hero took the King George V for the new King and Queen, giving them a first Royal Ascot winner, and went on to finish third in the St Leger in September.

Warm Heart, the Ribblesdale winner for Aidan O'Brien, scaled great heights with two Group 1 victories in Europe before landing the Grade 1 Pegasus World Cup Turf at Gulfstream Park in January.

Three year-old handicappers also feature in the Britannia Stakes, the second of the week's heritage handicaps and basically a Royal Hunt Cup for colts and geldings from the younger age group. A high-grade performer, often one capable of winning in Group company, is likely to emerge at the front of a maximum field of 30 down the straight mile.

Speed is injected by the Group 2 Norfolk Stakes for two-year-olds over the minimum trip of five furlongs. This contest lasts barely 60 seconds, compared with the near four and a half minutes it takes to complete the Gold Cup.

Race six is the Hampton Court Stakes, a Group 3 for three-year-olds over a mile and a quarter that also often showcases an emerging talent.

The final race is the Buckingham Palace Stakes, a seven-furlong handicap for three-year-olds and up which regained its place at the royal meeting in 2020 as part of the expansion to seven races per day.

Dating back to 1843, this is the meeting's third Group 2 race for two-year-olds, following the Coventry and Queen Mary Stakes, and its distinguishing feature is that it is open to both sexes over the minimum distance of five furlongs.

Last year's winner

Valiant Force at 150-1 equalled the record for the longest-priced winner at Royal Ascot, set by Nando Parrado in the 2020 Coventry Stakes, and not surprisingly came up short on trends, most notably lacking the usual winning form.

Form As this is often the major target for a speedy and precocious two-year-old, it is no surprise to find that most winners have been pushed

Key trends

▶ By a sire with a stamina index between 6.7f and 8.3f, nine winners in last ten runnings
▶ Won within last two starts, 8/10
▶ Top-three finish last time out, 8/10 (six won)
▶ Adjusted RPR of at least

100, 7/10
▶ Beaten on debut, 7/10 (all exceptions once-raced winners)

Other factors

▶ Only five winners had scored over 5f
▶ Six fillies have run in the last decade, finishing 990156

hard enough beforehand to achieve an adjusted RPR well into three figures and Valiant Force and A'Ali (2019) are the only maidens to take this prize since 1990.

Key races Most winners have not been highly tried, often running at mid-ranking tracks. Eleven of the last 25 winners had won their only start, with connections happy they had done enough before Ascot (another was unbeaten in three starts).

Trainers Along with the ever-dangerous Aidan O'Brien (three wins), trainers known for fast horses have done well, including Richard Fahey, Wesley Ward, Richard Hannon, Clive Cox, Kevin Ryan and Robert Cowell.

Betting The extent to which connections know what they have on their hands is clear from the winning odds over a long period, with only six of the last 25 winners going off bigger than 10-1.

Story of the last ten years

	FORM	WINNER	AGE & WGT	Adj RPR	SP	TRAINER	BEST RPR LAST 12 MONTHS (RUNS SINCE)
23	25	**Valiant Force**	2 9-3	100-19	150-1	Adrian Murray (IRE)	2nd Curragh Listed (5f) (1)
22	413	**The Ridler** D	2 9-3	102-11	50-1	Richard Fahey	3rd Beverley Class 2 conditions (5f) (0)
21	31	**Perfect Power** D	2 9-1	94-13	14-1	Richard Fahey	won Hamilton Class 5 maiden (5f) (0)
20	1	**The Lir Jet** D	2 9-1	100-3	9-2	Michael Bell	won Yarmouth Class 5 novice (5f) (0)
19	2	**A'Ali** BF	2 9-1	101-15	5-1	Simon Crisford	2nd Ripon Class 5 novice (5f) (0)
18	1	**Shang Shang Shang**	2 8-12	99-15	5-1	Wesley Ward (USA)	won Keeneland maiden (4½f) (0)
17	3216	**Sioux Nation**	2 9-1	103-10	14-1	Aidan O'Brien (IRE)	won Cork maiden (6f) (1)
16	1	**Prince Lir** D	2 9-1	105-11	8-1	Robert Cowell	won Beverley Class 2 conditions (5f) (0)
15	6321	**Waterloo Bridge** D	2 9-1	97-23	12-1	Aidan O'Brien (IRE)	won Tipperary maiden (5f) (0)
14	211	**Baitha Alga**	2 9-1	110-2	8-1	Richard Hannon	won Woodcote Stakes Listed (6f) (0)

FAVOURITES -£10.00

TRAINERS IN THIS RACE (w-pl-r): Aidan O'Brien 2-1-11, Richard Hannon 1-2-8, Wesley Ward 1-1-8, Richard Fahey 2-2-8, Robert Cowell 1-1-6, Michael Bell 1-0-2, William Haggas 0-0-2, Karl Burke 0-2-5, Andrew Balding 0-1-2, Clive Cox 0-0-4

FATE OF FAVOURITES 5352000423 **POSITION OF WINNER IN MARKET** 3359323690

First run at Royal Ascot in 1948, this is a fascinating yet tricky 1m4f handicap for three-year-olds, open to fillies as well as colts and geldings.

Last year's winner Desert Hero, owned by King Charles and Queen Camilla, went off at 18-1 but fitted key trends on rating, weight, handicap experience and draw.

Form Classy stayer Brown Panther in 2011 and Baghdad in 2018 are the only recent winners who had raced this far before but one clue to potential stamina can be gleaned from two-year-old form. The last winner who had been unraced at two was Heron Bay in 2007 and 14 of the 16 winners since had been tried over 1m-1m2f as juveniles (the other two had run at 7f and 7½f).

Draw Eight consecutive winners came from a double-figure stall up to 2018 but then there was a run of three out of four in single figures until Desert Hero scored from stall 21 last year. A low draw can be tricky but is not such an issue for a prominent racer.

Key races Seven winners in the past decade had been racing in handicaps and all but one had been successful in that sphere last time out.

Trainers The bigger stables tend to be well stocked with the right type of lightly raced challenger. Two to watch in this and other 1m4f races are Charlie Johnston (father Mark had six winners) and Sir Michael Stoute (four). Godolphin have won four of the past ten runnings (with three different trainers), while Aidan O'Brien has had a winner, a runner-up and a third in three of the last four editions where he had a representative.

Betting Since Cosmic Sun scored at 66-1 in 2009, eight of the 14 winners have come from the top four in the market.

Key trends

- *Officially rated between 88 and 95, 10/10*
- *Top-two finish last time, 9/10 (seven won)*
- *Carried no more than 9st 1lb, 8/10*
- *Previously contested a handicap, 8/10 (six won one)*
- *Won earlier in the season, 8/10*
- *Drawn in double figures, 7/10*

Other factors

- *The Johnston yard has had six winners since 1995, while Sir Michael Stoute has had four*
- *Only one winner had previously scored over the trip*

Story of the last ten years

	FORM	WINNER	AGE & WGT	OR	SP	TRAINER	BEST RPR LAST 12 MONTHS (RUNS SINCE)
23	131-8	**Desert Hero** BF	3 8-13	94-5	18-1	William Haggas	3rd Solario Stakes Group 3 (7f) (2)
22	211	**Secret State**	3 9-6	93ᵀ	4-1j	Charlie Appleby	won Nottingham Class 5 nov (1m½f) (0)
21	91-21	**Surefire** (6ex)	3 8-9	88-2	5-1	Ralph Beckett	won Leicester Class 4 hcap (1m2f) (0)
20	21-	**Hukum**	3 8-11	90-9	12-1	Owen Burrows	won Kempton Class 4 novice (1m) (0)
19	2-B12	**South Pacific** (1ow) BF	3 8-10	94-10	22-1	Aidan O'Brien (IRE)	2nd Naas rated (1m2f) (0)
18	41-31	**Baghdad** D	3 8-12	90-2	9-1	Mark Johnston	won York Class 4 handicap (1m4f) (0)
17	1-12	**Atty Persse** BF	3 8-7	93-2	7-1	Roger Charlton	2nd Haydock Class 3 hcap (1m2f) (0)
16	21-11	**Gold Mount**	3 9-3	95-3	13-2	Alan King	won Sandown Class 3 hcap (1m2f) (0)
15	31-51	**Space Age**	3 8-10	88ᵀ	9-1	Charlie Appleby	won Newmarket Class 3 hcap (1m2f) (0)
14	1-31	**Elite Army**	3 9-1	94-5	4-1j	Saeed bin Suroor	won Sandown Class 3 hcap (1m2f) (0)

FAVOURITES -£5.00 **FATE OF FAVOURITES:** 1000002215 **POSITION OF WINNER IN MARKET:** 1432508210

3.45 Ribblesdale Stakes

FIRST run in 1919, this 1m4f highlight is the meeting's premier race for middle-distance fillies from the Classic generation and often draws runners who have competed in the Oaks or at least the trials.

Last year's winner Warm Heart was on her way up for Aidan O'Brien, having won at Listed level last time, and scored here at 13-2 before taking a string of top-level successes capped by the Pegasus World Cup Turf at Gulfstream Park in January.

Form To a large extent this race draws still-developing fillies, with 11 of the last 12 winners having run no more than four times before this assignment, but most of them had shown enough ability to be tried in Pattern company. The top level might be beyond them at this stage but if you remove Group 1 runs that season from the records of the winners since 2010, they would show 16 wins, four seconds and four thirds from 24 runs.

Key races Five winners since 2010 had run in a Guineas or the Oaks, although none finished closer than fourth and that explains why they were going for this Group 2 rather than a top-level target. A placing in a minor Oaks or a trial is often a significant marker.

Trainers In the past 18 runnings the winner has come from Newmarket (ten) or Irish yards (eight).

Betting There have been some big-priced shocks over the years but only one of the last 17 winners was outside the top five in the betting, with ten of them in the top two.

Key trends

- ▶ Raced no more than three times at two, 10/10
- ▶ Adjusted RPR of at least 109, 10/10
- ▶ Contested a Listed or Group race, 9/10 (three had won a Group race)
- ▶ Won in last two starts, 7/10
- ▶ Won over at least 1m2f, 6/10

Other factors

- ▶ In 2022, Magical Lagoon was the first RPR top-rated winner since Banimpire in 2011. The other nine were between 5lb and 18lb off top
- ▶ Five winners failed to shed their maiden tag the previous season

Story of the last ten years

	FORM	WINNER	AGE & WGT	Adj RPR	SP	TRAINER	BEST RPR LAST 12 MONTHS (RUNS SINCE)
23	4-211	**Warm Heart**	3 9-2	109⁻¹⁸	13-2	Aidan O'Brien (IRE)	won Newbury Listed (1m2f) (0)
22	417-2	**Magical Lagoon**	3 9-2	119ᵀ	11-4	Jessica Harrington (IRE)	2nd Navan Listed (1m2f) (0)
21	71-25	**Loving Dream**	3 9-0	111⁻¹⁴	18-1	John & Thady Gosden	2nd Wetherby Class 5 maiden (1m2f) (1)
20	2-1	**Frankly Darling**	3 9-0	109⁻⁸	11-8f	John Gosden	won Newcastle Class 5 maiden (1m2f) (0)
19	6-13	**Star Catcher**	3 9-0	113⁻¹³	4-1	John Gosden	3rd Newbury Fillies' Trial (1m2f) (0)
18	7-314	**Magic Wand**	3 9-0	120⁻⁵	10-3	Aidan O'Brien (IRE)	won Cheshire Oaks Gp3 (1m3½f) (1)
17	11-35	**Coronet**	3 9-0	114⁻⁹	9-1	John Gosden	3rd Prix Saint-Alary Gp1 (1m2f) (1)
16	31-3	**Even Song**	3 9-0	113⁻¹⁶	15-8f	Aidan O'Brien (IRE)	3rd Newmarket Listed (1m2f) (0)
15	8-111	**Curvy**	3 9-0	122⁻⁵	9-2	David Wachman (IRE)	won Curragh Gp3 (1m2f) (0)
14	81-10	**Bracelet**	3 9-0	119⁻⁷	10-1	Aidan O'Brien (IRE)	won Leopardstown Gp3 (7f) (1)

FAVOURITES: -£4.75

TRAINERS IN THIS RACE (w-pl-r) Aidan O'Brien 4-3-17, John & Thady Gosden 1-0-6, Charlie Appleby 0-1-2, Jessica Harrington 1-0-2, Andrew Balding 0-0-2, Ralph Beckett 0-1-8, Roger Varian 0-2-6, Joseph O'Brien 0-1-2, William Haggas 0-1-5

FATE OF FAVOURITES: 4212221626 **POSITION OF WINNER IN MARKET:** 5214321823

Injured Jockeys Fund

Helping Jockeys
(Since 1964)
with your support

To donate please visit

www.ijf.org.uk

or call 01638 662246

You can also Text IJF to 70800 to donate £5

Compassion • Care • Support

Injured Jockeys Fund (Registered Charity No. 1107395)

DAY THREE

FOUNDED in 1807, this is one of the crown jewels of Royal Ascot and at two and a half miles is the premier staying race of the British Flat season.

Last year's winner
Courage Mon Ami arrived on a four-timer and was fourth favourite at 15-2 but, having last run in a Goodwood handicap, did not fit key trends on ratings, distance and established class.

Form The class factor is important, with 20 of the 24 winners since 2000 having previously struck in a Group 1 or Group 2 (15 had won at the highest level). Only follow-up winners Royal Rebel, Yeats and Stradivarius,

Frankie Dettori's flying dismount from Courage Mon Ami last year along with 2005 winner Westerner, had scored at this trip before, but just five (four trained by Aidan O'Brien, plus Courage Mon Ami) had yet to win over at least 2m.

Key races There is not a wide choice of targets for stayers and many recent winners have come down the Sagaro/Henry II/Yorkshire Cup route in Britain or via the Vintage Crop/Saval Beg in Ireland. Ten of the last 17 winners had won at least one of those races en route and another had been runner-up in the Henry II. The previous year's Gold Cup is also a guide – ten horses have won the race more than once in the near half-century since Sagaro, one of the greats, started his hat-trick in 1975.

Trainers O'Brien has been the dominant force in recent years. He has won eight of the last 18 runnings with five different horses. His only multiple scorer is Yeats, who is still out on his own as a

Key trends
▶ *Sire stamina index in excess of 9.5f, 10/10*
▶ *Won within last two starts, 9/10*
▶ *Adjusted RPR of at least 127, 8/10*
▶ *Group-race winner, 8/10 (six had won a Group 1)*
▶ *Won over at least 2m, 7/10*
▶ *Rated within 8lb of RPR top-rated, 8/10 (four were top-rated)*

Other factors
▶ *Eight winners were competing in the race for the first time (Stradivarius in 2019 and 2020 accounts for both exceptions)*
▶ *Winners of the Sagaro Stakes finished 727322462 – the last to succeed was Estimate in 2013*
▶ *Six favourites have won in the last decade (including*

four-time winner (2006-2009).

Betting Fancied runners have an excellent record.

one joint-favourite) but Stradivarius was the only one to have previously scored over the trip

Roll of honour
Longest-priced winner
25-1 Indian Queen (1991)

Shortest-priced winner
1-5 Ardross (1981)

Most successful trainer
8 wins: **Aidan O'Brien**
Yeats (2006, 2007, 2008, 2009), Fame And Glory (2011), Leading Light (2014), Order Of St George (2016), Kyprios (2022)

Most successful jockey
11 wins: **Lester Piggott**
Zarathustra (1957), Gladness (1958), Pandofell (1961), Twilight Alley (1963), Fighting Charlie (1965), Sagaro (1975, 1976, 1977), Le Moss (1979), Ardross (1981, 1982)

Most successful owner
7 wins: **Coolmore partners**
Yeats (2006, 2007, 2008, 2009), Fame And Glory (2011), Leading Light (2014), Order Of St George (2016)

*All figures since 1946

Only three of the 24 winners since 2000 were outside the top four in the market and 16 were in the top two.

Story of the last ten years

	FORM	WINNER	AGE & WGT	Adj RPR	SP	TRAINER	BEST RPR LAST 12 MONTHS (RUNS SINCE)
23	11-1	**Courage Mon Ami**	4 9-3	123-8	15-2	John & Thady Gosden	won Goodwood Class 2 hcap (1m6f) (0)
22	14-11	**Kyprios**	4 9-3	130-2	13-8f	Aidan O'Brien (IRE)	won Saval Beg Stakes Gp3 (1m6f) (0)
21	171-1	**Subjectivist**	4 9-1	127-10	13-2	Mark Johnston	won Dubai Gold Cup Gp2 (2m) (0)
20	112-3	**Stradivarius** CD	6 9-2	135T	4-5f	John Gosden	won Goodwood Cup Gp1 (2m) (4)
19	111-1	**Stradivarius** CD	5 9-2	133T	Evsf	John Gosden	won Goodwood Cup Gp1 (2m) (3)
18	133-1	**Stradivarius** C	4 9-1	132-5	7-4j	John Gosden	3rd St Leger Gp1 (1m6½f) (2)
17	30-41	**Big Orange** C	6 9-2	131-3	5-1	Michael Bell	won Princess of Wales's Gp2 (1m4f) (6)
16	111-1	**Order Of St George**	4 9-0	137T	10-11f	Aidan O'Brien (IRE)	won Irish St Leger Gp1 (1m6f) (1)
15	41112	**Trip To Paris** C	4 9-0	121-10	12-1	Ed Dunlop	2nd Henry II Stakes Gp3 (2m) (0)
14	110-1	**Leading Light** C	4 9-0	133T	10-11f	Aidan O'Brien (IRE)	won Vintage Crop Stakes Gp3 (1m6f) (0)

WINS-RUNS 4yo 7-6-43, 5yo 1-5-25, 6yo+ 2-9-49 **FAVOURITES** £1.62

TRAINERS IN THIS RACE Aidan O'Brien 3-2-14, John & Thady Gosden 1-1-3, Andrew Balding 0-2-8, Willie Mullins 0-0-7, Hughie Morrison 0-0-4, Ralph Beckett 0-0-4, Ian Williams 0-0-1, Christophe Ferland 0-0-1

FATE OF FAVOURITES 1312111412 **POSITION OF WINNER IN MARKET** 1612111214

FIRST run in 1928, this contest over the straight mile is the second of Royal Ascot's three heritage handicaps and is open to three-year-old colts and geldings.

Last year's winner

Docklands fitted every key trend and duly delivered as 6-1 favourite for Harry Eustace, giving him a second Royal Ascot handicap winner after Latin Lover in the 2022 Palace of Holyroodhouse.

Form A good level of form is important, with Docklands top on Racing Post Ratings last year. Most winners have been lightly raced, with seven of the last ten having had no more than four outings. Getting in on a weight just below 9st might be ideal, with 12 of the last 20 winners having been in the range from 8st 8lb to 8st 13lb.

Key trends
▶ *At least one top-three finish within last two starts, 9/10*
▶ *Drawn in double figures, 9/10*
▶ *Officially rated between 90 and 99, 8/10*
▶ *Carried no more than 9st 2lb, 8/10*
▶ *Won in current season over 7f or a mile, 7/10*
▶ *Rated within 6lb of RPR top-rated, 7/10 (three were top-rated)*
▶ *Previously contested a handicap, 6/10*

Other factors
▶ *Four winners had previously won a handicap, while another four were making their handicap debut*
▶ *The Gosden yard hasn't won this for a while, but was successful four times between 1996 and 2001*

Draw Six of the last ten winners have been in the middle third (stalls 11-20) and only one was lower than that. An experienced, tactically astute jockey is an advantage.

Key races Most winners had been restricted to maiden, novice and latterly handicap company, with six winners in the past decade having run in a handicap before coming here (four had won a handicap).

Trainers The only repeat winner in the last 20 runnings is the now-retired Roger Charlton (successful with Fifteen Love in 2008 and again in partnership with son Harry with Thesis in 2022).

Betting Five winners in the past decade were sent off at 14-1 or bigger and Docklands was only the second winning favourite since 2006.

Story of the last ten years

	FORM	WINNER	AGE	& WGT	OR	SP	TRAINER	BEST RPR LAST 12 MONTHS (RUNS SINCE)
23	2-211	**Docklands** CD	3	9-2	94^T	6-1f	Harry Eustace	won Ascot Class 4 handicap (1m) (0)
22	3-222	**Thesis** BF	3	8-11	90^5	14-1	Harry & Roger Charlton	2nd Doncaster Class 5 novice (7f) (0)
21	3-241	**Perotto** (5ex)	3	9-3	99^8	18-1	Marcus Tregoning	2nd Newmarket Class 2 handicap (6f) (2)
20	21	**Khaloosy**	3	9-2	94^17	9-2	Roger Varian	won Wolver Class 5 novice (1m½f) (0)
19	112	**Biometric** BF	3	8-8	92^7	28-1	Ralph Beckett	won Newbury Class 4 novice (7f) (1)
18	2-221	**Ostilio** D	3	8-9	90^3	10-1	Simon Crisford	won Newmarket Class 4 hcap (1m) (0)
17	2135	**Bless Him** D	3	8-9	90^6	25-1	David Simcock	5th Goodwood Class 2 hcap (7f) (0)
16	3-141	**Limitless** D	3	9-1	95^T	13-2	Jamie Osborne	won Doncaster Class 4 hcap (1m) (0)
15	-2470	**War Envoy**	3	9-6	104^T	10-1	Aidan O'Brien (IRE)	5th Prix Jean-Luc Lagardere Gp1 (7f) (5)
14	312	**Born In China** D	3	8-4	87^-1	14-1	Andrew Balding	2nd Newmarket Class 2 hcap (1m) (0)

FAVOURITES -£3.00

FATE OF FAVOURITES 4060022901 **POSITION OF WINNER IN MARKET** 6430502771

ASCOT TOP HATS

FABER CAUSIARUM ALTARUM

TM

At **Ascot Top Hats Ltd**, we provide new felt Toppers and Vintage Silk Top Hats, as well as refurbishment and fitting services to reshape hats to heads to make them comfortable.

Ascot Top Hats Ltd

By appointment at our workshop please call:
01344 638 838 www.ascot-tophats.co.uk

Unit 24 Space Business Centre,
Molly Millars Lane, Wokingham, Berks RG41 2PQ

Ascot Top Hats Ltd is a company registered in England and Wales
Incorporation Number: 5740259 Registered Office: Beechey House,
87 Church Street, Crowthorne, Berkshire, RG45 7AW

5.40 Hampton Court Stakes

THIS Group 3 race for three-year-olds was added to the programme when Royal Ascot was extended to five days in 2002 and upgraded to its current level in 2011.

Last year's winner

Waipiro struck at 7-1 for Ed Walker, having arrived with most of the key boxes ticked and with a last-time-out Derby sixth on his record.

Form Five of the 22 winners since 2002 were unraced as two-year-olds and another seven had failed to win at that age. A last-time-out success is a good pointer, although failure to win can be more readily excused if that run was in a Classic or another Group 1.

Key races There are two main routes to this race – either through handicaps

Key trends
- ▶ *Yet to win at this level or higher, 10/10*
- ▶ *Adjusted RPR of at least 120, 9/10*
- ▶ *Rated within 7lb of RPR top-rated, 8/10 (four were top-rated)*
- ▶ *Won that season, 8/10*
- ▶ *Top-three finish last time out, 6/10 (four won)*
- ▶ *Distance winner, 6/10*

Other factors
- ▶ *Two had won a handicap that season*
- ▶ *Six had been beaten in Classic trials*

(two of the last ten winners) or principally from the Classic trail. In 2020 Russian Emperor was en route to the Derby (run after Royal Ascot that year), where he was seventh; in 2021 Mohaafeth came here after being a Derby non-runner due to the

ground; and in 2022 Claymore had been second in the Craven Stakes before finishing last from a poor draw in the French 2,000 Guineas. Last year Waipiro was runner-up in the Lingfield Derby Trial before his Epsom sixth.

Trainers The roll of honour is dominated by the big yards that house plenty of later-developing three-year-olds, with 13 of the last 16 winners having come from Newmarket or Aidan O'Brien's Ballydoyle stable. O'Brien had the third in 2016, the second and fourth in 2017, the winner in 2018 and 2020 and the runner-up in 2021.

Betting Most winners had done enough to take high rank in the betting, with none of the last 12 winners priced at bigger than 7-1.

Story of the last ten years

	FORM	WINNER		AGE & WGT	Adj RPR	SP	TRAINER	BEST RPR LAST 12 MONTHS (RUNS SINCE)
23	6-126	**Waipiro** D		3 9-2	121-7	7-1	Ed Walker	2nd Lingfield Derby Trial (1m4f) (0)
22	1-20	**Claymore**		3 9-2	121-8	7-1	Jane Chapple-Hyam	2nd Craven Stakes Gp3 (1m) (1)
21	3-111	**Mohaafeth** D		3 9-0	131T	11-8f	William Haggas	won Newmarket Listed (1m2f) (0)
20	3-12	**Russian Emperor** BF		3 9-0	98-28	10-3	Aidan O'Brien (IRE)	2nd Leopardstown Gp3 (1m2f) (0)
19	114-3	**Sangarius**		3 9-0	120-6	13-2	Sir Michael Stoute	3rd Sandown Listed (1m) (0)
18	-1336	**Hunting Horn** D		3 9-0	124T	5-1	Aidan O'Brien (IRE)	6th Prix du Jockey Club (1m2½f) (0)
17	1325	**Benbatl**		3 9-0	128T	9-2	Saeed bin Suroor	5th Derby Gp1 (1m4f) (0)
16	111-1	**Hawkbill** D		3 9-0	121-4	11-2	Charlie Appleby	won Newmarket Listed (1m2f) (0)
15	212-1	**Time Test** D		3 9-0	123T	15-8f	Roger Charlton	won Newbury Class 2 hcap (1m2f) (0)
14	2-11	**Cannock Chase** D		3 9-0	122-1	7-4f	Sir Michael Stoute	won Newbury Class 2 hcap (1m2f) (0)

FAVOURITES -£2.00

TRAINERS IN THIS RACE (w-pl-r) Sir Michael Stoute 2-3-8, Aidan O'Brien 2-3-13, Saeed bin Suroor 1-1-6, Charlie Appleby 1-2-7, William Haggas 1-1-2, Jane Chapple-Hyam 1-0-1, Roger Varian 0-1-4, John & Thady Gosden 0-1-4, Ralph Beckett 0-0-1

FATE OF FAVOURITES 1122622124 **POSITION OF WINNER IN MARKET** 1142242124

ORIGINALLY introduced to the expanded royal meeting in 2002, this big-field seven-furlong handicap for three-year-olds and upwards was removed after 2014 to make room for the new Group 1 Commonwealth Cup but reinstated in 2020 as part of the extended race programme.

Last year's winner Witch Hunter reiterated this race's propensity for big-priced winners when he struck at 50-1 for Richard Hannon, even though he was ridden by straight-track handicap maestro Jamie Spencer. He had some plus points on trends but was high in the ratings and ran off near top weight of 9st 10lb.

Form This tends to favour a progressive type who gets in on a mid-range weight. In the four runnings since the race's resumption, all bar two of the first three places have gone to a four-year-old. Good form in a big-field handicap is a positive pointer.

(Removed from the meeting after 2014; reintroduced in 2020)

Key trends
▶ *At least one top-three finish within last three starts 5/5*
▶ *Officially rated 92 to 99, 4/5*
▶ *Carried no more than 9st 4lb, 4/5*
▶ *Aged four, 4/5*
▶ *Won in a field with at least 11 runners, 4/5*
▶ *Distance winner, 3/5*

Other factors
▶ *All five winners were priced between 12-1 and 50-1*

Draw A high draw is often an advantage. The last six winners came from stalls 32, 29, 26, 31, 2 and 24.

Key races The Victoria Cup over the same course and distance in May is an obvious stepping stone (last used successfully by Louis The Pious in 2014). Recent 7f/1m handicaps at Newmarket, Haydock and York are worth checking.

Trainers The only trainers to have won more than once are Kevin Ryan (Uhoomagoo in 2006 and Lightning Cloud in 2013) and Hannon (Motakhayyel in 2020 and Witch Hunter last year).

Betting There has never been a successful favourite in the 17 runnings and the only winners not at double-figure odds were 8-1 shots Unscrupulous (2004) and Jedburgh (2005).

Witch Hunter: second winner in four years for Richard Hannon

Story of recent years

	FORM	WINNER	AGE	& WGT	OR	SP	TRAINER	BEST RPR LAST 12 MONTHS (RUNS SINCE)
23	02025	**Witch Hunter** D	4	9-10	103-11	50-1	Richard Hannon	2nd Newcastle Class 2 cond (6f) (3)
22	-2311	**Inver Park** C	4	9-1	94-2	12-1	George Boughey	won Hamilton Class 4 hcap (6f) (0)
21	0-312	**Highfield Princess** D, BF	4	8-11	92-3	18-1	John Quinn	won Haydock Class 4 hcap (7f) (1)
20	1216-	**Motakhayyel** D	4	9-3	98-6	14-1	Richard Hannon	won Newmarket Class2 hcap (1m) (1)
14	9-720	**Louis The Pious**	6	9-4	99-4	33-1	David O'Meara	2nd Haydock Class 2 hcap (7f) (1)

WINS-RUNS 3yo 0-0-1, 4yo 4-9-59, 5yo 0-4-33, 6yo+ 1-2-44 **FAVOURITES** -£5.00

FATE OF FAVOURITES: 00559 **POSITION OF WINNER IN MARKET:** 06860

EXPERT VIEW

Racing Post Ratings handicapper Matt Gardner picks
six horses who look set to run big races at Royal Ascot

ALBASHEER

6yo gelding
Trainer: Archie Watson
RPR 117

Rohaan; the Wokingham winner in 2021 and 2022, appears to have been primed for another crack at the 6f handicap and makes the shortlist but Albasheer may be even better handicapped. He thrived after joining Archie Watson last year, winning at York's Ebor meeting (in a dead-heat) and shaping well in several other competitive handicaps. He improved on the all-weather over the winter, posting a pair of career-best efforts at Newcastle, and there's little reason to think he can't translate that form back to turf, with the handicapper taking a real chance by leaving his turf mark of 100 unchanged.

NOTABLE SPEECH

3yo colt
Charlie Appleby
RPR 123

The best bet of the meeting may well be Notable Speech in the St James's Palace Stakes. He's had a remarkable rise from winning a Kempton maiden in January to 2,000 Guineas victory and his Newmarket performance ranked highly among recent winners, bettered only by Gleneagles in the last ten years. It's difficult to envisage anything behind him at Newmarket reversing the form, not least with Notable Speech capable of better still in all likelihood.

PASSENGER

4yo colt
Sir Michael Stoute
RPR 122

This time last year Passenger was in the midst of a Derby campaign, having arguably shaped like the best horse when third in the Dante. His inexperience was highlighted at Epsom, which came just six weeks after his debut in the Wood Ditton, but he got back on track in Windsor's Winter Hill Stakes on his only other start last year and looked full of promise again when winning the Huxley Stakes on his reappearance this term, putting him in line for a return to Group 1 company in the Prince of Wales's Stakes. Given how

well similar types have responded to his trainer's signature patient approach in the past, it's likely that Passenger's best days are still ahead of him.

PEARLE D'OR

5yo gelding
David O'Meara
RPR 98

It's well worth keeping the faith with Pearle D'Or in competitive, big-field handicaps and the Buckingham Palace appears to be tailor-made for him. His Ascot record over 7f is excellent with form figures of 213 in three starts last year. He ran much better than the result indicated when well backed in the Victoria Cup over course and distance in May,

meeting trouble before finding himself marooned on the far side while the principals were on the near side. He'll need some luck but is well enough handicapped to win a race of this nature.

TWILIGHT CALLS

6yo gelding
Henry Candy
RPR 115

There's an open feel to the newly named King Charles III Stakes this year with nothing particularly standing out on form, perhaps granting the opportunity for a perennial nearly horse to make the breakthrough at the top level. Twilight Calls finished second in the race in 2022 but it was his eyecatching run last year, when fourth behind Bradsell, that really suggested he'd be capable of winning a big one when

things drop right. His encouraging reappearance at Newmarket shows the fire still burns brightly in his fifth year of racing.

WHISTLEJACKET

2yo colt
Aidan O'Brien
RPR 101

Whistlejacket became the early front-runner on Racing Post Ratings among the juveniles when winning a five-runner Listed race at the Curragh in early May, beating three previous winners and a well-bred newcomer by an impressive three and three-quarters of a length. The half-brother to Little Big Bear (who won the Windsor Castle in 2022) looks all speed and ought to be really well suited to the Norfolk Stakes, with his form already not far off the standard it usually takes to win that race.

Albasheer: this winter's all-weather improver looks well handicapped for the Wokingham

DAY FOUR

Friday's change of order moves the Coronation Stakes up a place to the third race, putting the two Group 1 highlights back to back on another stellar card. After Tuesday's opening salvo, this is the only other day with more than one Group 1 contest.

The Coronation, over a mile for three-year-old fillies, is the traditional Friday centrepiece and often attracts graduates from the 1,000 Guineas, Irish 1,000 Guineas and Poule d'Essai des Pouliches in a clash that can sort out the Classic form. Victory last year went to Irish Guineas winner Tahiyra.

The first Group 1 on the card is the Commonwealth Cup, which will have its tenth running this year. Its introduction has been an unqualified success, offering an early top-level opportunity for three-year-old sprinters without having to take on their elders, and the standard was set in the first year when it was won by champion sprinter Muhaarar.

Shaquille was another high-class Commonwealth winner last year before going on to add the Group 1 July Cup at Newmarket three weeks later.

Classic form is also on show in the King Edward VII Stakes, the only Group 2 on the card. Often called the Ascot Derby, this mile-and-

a-half race regularly attracts horses who have participated in the premier Classic at Epsom.

Last year's race went to King Of Steel, who had been a half-length runner-up in the Derby on his seasonal debut three weeks earlier. He rounded off his season with Group 1 victory in the Champion Stakes back at Ascot, while King Edward VII runner-up Continuous went on to take the St Leger.

Friday's card opens with the Group 3 Albany Stakes, the first of three races on the day restricted to fillies. Last year's winner was Porta

Fortuna, who went on to take the Group 1 Cheveley Park Stakes and finish a close runner-up both in the Breeders' Cup Juvenile Fillies Turf and this year's 1,000 Guineas.

The first handicap on the card is the Duke of Edinburgh Stakes for three-year-olds and up over a mile and a half. After that comes the Sandringham Stakes, a hotly contested handicap for three-year-old fillies over the straight mile, and the card is completed by the Palace of Holyroodhouse Stakes, a five-furlong handicap for three-year-olds.

Friday June 21

RUNNING ORDER

2.30 **Albany Stakes** (Group 3) Last year's winner: Porta Fortuna 5-1	**6f** 2yo fillies	£125,000
3.05 **Commonwealth Cup** (Group 1) Last year's winner: Shaquille 9-1	**6f** 3yo colts and fillies	£650,000
3.45 **Coronation Stakes** (Group 1) Last year's winner: Tahiyra 8-13f	**1m** 3yo fillies	£650,000
4.25 **Duke of Edinburgh Stakes** (Handicap) Last year's winner: Okita Soushi 9-1	**1m4f** 3yo+	£110,000
5.05 **Sandringham Stakes** (Handicap) Last year's winner: Coppice 6-1jf	**1m** 3yo fillies	£110,000
5.40 **King Edward VII Stakes** (Group 2) Last year's winner: King Of Steel 11-10f	**1m4f** 3yo colts and geldings	£250,000
6.15 **Palace of Holyroodhouse Stakes** (H'cap) Last year's winner: Rhythm N Hooves 12-1	**5f** 3yo Race value is total prize-money	£110,000

ESTABLISHED in 2002 at Listed level and upgraded in 2005, this Group 3 6f contest is a two-year-old fillies' version of the Coventry Stakes, albeit without such a long history.

Last year's winner Porta Fortuna, already a Group 3 winner, scored here at 5-1 for Donnacha O'Brien before going on to Group 1 success in the Cheveley Park at Newmarket and a close second in the Grade 1 Breeders' Cup Juvenile Fillies Turf at Santa Anita and this year's 1,000 Guineas.

Form All of the last ten winners had won at least once (five came here after just one run) and an adjusted RPR of at least 96 has been essential during that period, indicating a good standard is required.

Key trends
▶ *No more than two runs, ten winners in last ten runnings*
▶ *At least 7lb off top-rated, 8/10 (last two top-rated winners the exceptions)*
▶ *Adjusted Racing Post Rating of at least 98, 8/10*
▶ *Distance winner, 8/10*
▶ *By a sire with a stamina index of at least 7.4f, 7/10*
▶ *Ran in maiden/novice last time out, 6/10*

Other factors
▶ *All of the last ten winners had scored last time out. The last maiden to win was Samitar in 2011*
▶ *Five were once-raced winners*
▶ *Seven winners were drawn 13 or higher, but the last three were in single figures*

Key races Victory in a Newmarket or Goodwood maiden/novice is a good sign and three of the last ten winners were once-raced all-weather scorers. Winning a Curragh maiden (as Porta Fortuna did last year) tends to be the first step for an Irish challenger.

Trainers The only trainers with more than one winner in the past decade are Roger Varian (Cursory Glance in 2014 and Daahyeh in 2019) and Aidan O'Brien (Brave Anna in 2016 and Meditate in 2022).

Betting This has not been a great race for favourites. Since Cuis Ghaire triumphed at 8-11 in 2008, only three market leaders have been successful. Four of the last ten winners have been returned at odds of 14-1 or bigger.

Story of the last ten years

	FORM	WINNER	AGE & WGT	Adj RPR	SP	TRAINER	BEST RPR LAST 12 MONTHS (RUNS SINCE)
23	11	**Porta Fortuna** D	2 9-2	113^T	5-1	Donnacha O'Brien (IRE)	won Naas Gp3 (6f) (0)
22	11	**Meditate** D	2 9-2	110^T	5-2	Aidan O'Brien (IRE)	won Naas Gp3 (6f) (0)
21	1	**Sandrine** D	2 9-0	102$^{.8}$	16-1	Andrew Balding	won Kempton Class 5 novice (5f) (0)
20	1	**Dandalla** D	2 9-0	96$^{.7}$	13-2	Karl Burke	won Newcastle Class 5 maiden (5f) (0)
19	1	**Daahyeh** D	2 9-0	105$^{.7}$	4-1f	Roger Varian	won Newmarket Class 4 novice (6f) (0)
18	11	**Main Edition** D	2 9-0	104$^{.7}$	7-1	Mark Johnston	won Goodwood Class 5 novice (6f) (0)
17	11	**Different League** D	2 9-0	96$^{.18}$	20-1	Matthieu Palussiere (FR)	won Angers conditions stakes (6f) (0)
16	81	**Brave Anna** D	2 9-0	103$^{.14}$	16-1	Aidan O'Brien (IRE)	won Curragh maiden (6f) (0)
15	1	**Illuminate** D	2 9-0	98$^{.12}$	4-1f	Richard Hannon	won Salisbury Class 3 conditions (5f) (0)
14	1	**Cursory Glance** D	2 9-0	98$^{.10}$	14-1	Roger Varian	won Kempton Class 5 maiden (6f) (0)

FAVOURITES £0.00

TRAINERS IN THIS RACE (w-pl-r) Roger Varian 2-1-6, Aidan O'Brien 2-3-13, Richard Hannon 1-0-10, Andrew Balding 1-0-2, Karl Burke 1-0-3, Charlie Hills 0-0-3, John & Thady Gosden 0-0-2, Wesley Ward 0-1-0, Charlie Appleby 0-1-4

FATE OF FAVOURITES 3152012028 **POSITION OF WINNER IN MARKET** 7179314922

NATIONAL HORSERACING MUSEUM

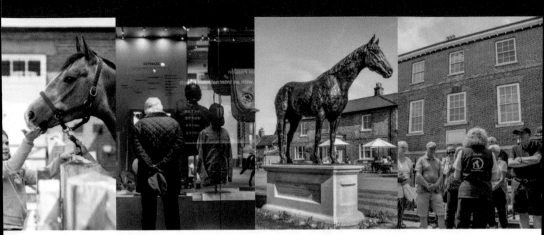

SO MUCH MORE THAN A MUSEUM!

Situated in the heart of Newmarket, the National Horseracing Museum allows you to immerse yourself in the history of horseracing, whilst enjoying some of the best examples of British sporting art in Palace House, as well as meet former racehorses in the Rothschild Yard.

This beautiful 5-acre site provides a wonderful day out for all ages!

Open Tuesday - Sunday | 01638 667314

@nhrmuseum      www.nhrm.co.uk

National Horseracing Museum Palace Street, Newmarket, Suffolk, CB8 8EP

THIS 6f sprint for three-year-olds was introduced in 2015, with the aim of allowing them to compete at the top level against their contemporaries without having to take on older horses at such an early stage of the season, and has proved a huge success.

Last year's winner
Shaquille wasn't yet a Group winner but was clearly improving fast for Julie Camacho and was joint-second on Racing Post Ratings. He scored at 9-1 from odds-on favourite Little Big Bear before going on to more Group 1 success in the July Cup three weeks later.

Form Most winners had plenty of proven form in Group company – in one or more two-year-old races over 5f and 6f, or in that year's early sprints. As a result of their achievements before Royal Ascot, all bar one of the nine winners were no more than 4lb off the top on RPR (the adjusted figure for eight of the nine was at least 128).

Key races Inaugural winner Muhaarar set the standard, having landed the Group 2 Gimcrack Stakes at York during his two-year-old career before taking the Group 3 Greenham Stakes on his reappearance at three. The Prix Morny, Middle Park, Dewhurst and Cornwallis

Key trends
▶ At least one top-two finish within last two starts, 9/9
▶ Distance winner, 9/9
▶ Adjusted RPR of at least 128, 8/9
▶ Rated within 4lb of RPR top-rated, 8/9 (three top-rated)
▶ Group-race winner, 7/9
▶ Drawn in single figures, 7/9
▶ Top-three finish at the track, 6/9

Other factors
▶ Three winners contested the Coventry the previous season, finishing 125. One had won the Queen Mary, while another landed the Norfolk
▶ Two had run in the 2,000 Guineas and one in the French Guineas (all comfortably beaten)
▶ 34 fillies have run, finishing 390001457000 252500098643135790 3460

Roll of honour
Longest-priced winner
12-1 Eqtidaar (2018)

Shortest-priced winner
5-6 Caravaggio (2017)

Most successful trainer
No multiple winners

Most successful jockey
2 wins: **Frankie Dettori**
Advertise (2019), Campanelle (2021)

Most successful owner
2 wins: **Hamdan Al Maktoum**
Muhaarar (2015), Eqtidaar (2018)

*All figures since 2015

Stakes have featured on the CVs of other winners.

Trainers No trainer has won more than once, but it is no surprise that the names of Charlie Hills, Karl Burke, Clive Cox, Wesley Ward and Richard Fahey (all adept with sprinters) on the roll of honour.

Betting Fancied horses have done well, with five of the nine winners coming from the top three in the market.

3.05 Commonwealth Cup

Last year's winner Shaquille with trainer Julie Camacho and her husband Steve Brown and work-rider Page Harrison

Story of the last nine years

	FORM	WINNER	AGE & WGT	Adj RPR	SP	TRAINER	BEST RPR LAST 12 MONTHS (RUNS SINCE)
23	11-11	**Shaquille** D	3 9-2	131⁻⁴	9-1	Julie Camacho	won Newbury Listed (6f) (0)
22	11-17	**Perfect Power** C, D	3 9-2	130ᵀ	7-2j	Richard Fahey	won Prix Morny Gp1 (6f) (3)
21	1114-	**Campanelle** C, D	3 8-11	131⁻¹	5-1	Wesley Ward (USA)	won Prix Morny Gp1 (6f) (1)
20	5132-	**Golden Horde** D	3 9-0	130⁻³	5-1	Clive Cox	2nd Middle Park Stakes Gp1 (6f) (0)
19	112-0	**Advertise** D	3 9-3	128⁻³	8-1	Martyn Meade	2nd Dewhurst Stakes Gp1 (7f) (1)
18	14-24	**Eqtidaar** D	3 9-3	118⁻⁹	12-1	Sir Michael Stoute	2nd Pavilion Stakes Gp3 (6f) (1)
17	111-1	**Caravaggio** CD	3 9-3	131ᵀ	5-6f	Aidan O'Brien (IRE)	won Lacken Stakes Gp3 (6f) (0)
16	11-11	**Quiet Reflection** D	3 9-0	130ᵀ	7-4f	Karl Burke	won Sandy Lane Stakes Gp2 (6f) (0)
15	13-18	**Muhaarar** D	3 9-3	128⁻³	10-1	Charlie Hills	won Greenham Stakes Gp3 (7f) (1)

FAVOURITES -£2.17

TRAINERS IN THIS RACE (w-pl-r) Aidan O'Brien 1-2-15, Karl Burke 1-1-6, Charlie Hills 1-0-5, Clive Cox 1-1-8, Wesley Ward 1-1-4, Richard Fahey 1-2-4, Charlie Appleby 0-1-6, Archie Watson 0-1-2, William Haggas 0-0-2, Roger Varian 0-0-5

FATE OF FAVOURITES 011040012 **POSITION OF WINNER IN MARKET** 611553314

DAY FOUR

FOUNDED to commemorate the crowning of Queen Victoria in 1838 and first run in 1840, this is the premier race for three-year-old fillies at Royal Ascot and, like the St James's Palace Stakes for colts on day one, often features a clash between the major Guineas winners.

Last year's winner

Tahiyra, a somewhat unlucky runner-up in the 1,000 Guineas at Newmarket before taking the Irish 1,000, did not have to face another Classic winner (Newmarket scorer Mawj headed off on a successful US campaign) and proved a cut above with victory by a length at 8-13.

Form A high level of form at two and/or in the spring Classics is paramount. With any runner who hasn't won a Guineas, the next best indicator is a Group 1 placing at two – 20 of the 24 winners since 2000 fell into one of those two categories. Fourteen of the 24 were either a Guineas winner or a Group 1 winner at two, although only 2013 winner Sky Lantern and Tahiyra last year were both.

Key races It is a regular occurrence for the Guineas participants from Britain, Ireland and France to go head to head here. All but three of the 24 winners since 2000 had run in a Guineas,

with eight having been successful in at least one of those Classics and four more placed.

Trainers Sir Michael Stoute, who landed his first Coronation with the brilliant Sonic Lady in 1986, has won four times, while Aidan O'Brien and the Gosden stable have been successful on three occasions. This race is an international draw and ten of the last 16 winners were trained outside Britain (six in Ireland, four in France). This is not the only time in the race's history

when overseas raiders have been to the fore. During the period 1989-1996 the race was won by French stables on three occasions (Andre Fabre, Criquette Head and Elie Lellouche) and two Irish yards (Michael Kauntze and John Oxx).

Betting Since 2000, Fallen For You (2012) and Watch Me (2019) are the only winners who weren't in the first four in the betting and the only ones sent off bigger than 8-1. Half of the 24 winners in that period were favourite or joint-favourite.

3.45 Coronation Stakes

Key trends
▶ *Adjusted RPR of at least 121, 10/10*
▶ *Rated within 7lb of RPR top-rated, 9/10*
▶ *Ran in a European 1,000 Guineas, 8/10*
▶ *Won earlier in the season, 7/10*

Other factors
▶ *Four winners had run in the 1,000 Guineas, where they finished 7152; three ran in France (136) and three in Ireland (111)*
▶ *Winners of the Irish 1,000 Guineas finished 611281*

Roll of honour
Longest-priced winner
25-1 Rebecca Sharp (1997)

Shortest-priced winner
1-6 Humble Duty (1970)

*All figures since 1946

Most successful trainer
5 wins: **Sir Henry Cecil**
Roussalka (1975), One In A Million (1979), Chalon (1982), Chimes Of Freedom (1990), Kissing Cousin (1994)

Most successful jockeys
4 wins: **Joe Mercer**
Festoon (1954), Rosalba (1959), Haymaking (1966), One In A Million (1979)

Lester Piggott
Aiming High (1961), Lisadell (1974), Roussalka (1975), Chalon (1982)

Walter Swinburn
Sonic Lady (1986), Milligram (1987), Marling (1992), Exclusive (1998)

Most successful owners
4 wins: **Niarchos family**
Magic Of Life (1988), Chimes Of Freedom (1990), Alpha Centauri (2018), Alpine Star (2020)

Cheveley Park Stud
Exclusive (1998), Russian Rhythm (2003), Nannina (2006), Inspiral (2022)

Chris Hayes celebrates Coronation victory 12 months ago on Tahiyra

Story of the last ten years

	FORM	WINNER	AGE & WGT	Adj RPR	SP	TRAINER	BEST RPR LAST 12 MONTHS (RUNS SINCE)
23	11-21	**Tahiyra** D	3 9-2	129^T	8-13f	Dermot Weld (IRE)	won Moyglare Stud Stakes Gp1 (7f) (2)
22	1111-	**Inspiral** D	3 9-2	128^T	15-8f	John & Thady Gosden	won Fillies' Mile Gp1 (1m) (0)
21	21-15	**Alcohol Free** BF	3 9-0	127^{-1}	11-2	Andrew Balding	won Cheveley Park Stakes Gp1 (6f) (2)
20	311-	**Alpine Star**	3 9-0	122^{-7}	9-2	Jessica Harrington (IRE)	won Debutante Stakes Gp2 (7f) (0)
19	31-16	**Watch Me** D	3 9-0	121^{-10}	20-1	Francis Graffard (FR)	won Prix Imprudence Gp3 (7f) (1)
18	25-01	**Alpha Centauri** D	3 9-0	128^{-1}	11-4f	Jessica Harrington (IRE)	won Irish 1,000 Guineas Gp1 (1m) (0)
17	1-211	**Winter** D	3 9-0	133^T	4-9f	Aidan O'Brien (IRE)	won Irish 1,000 Guineas Gp1 (1m) (0)
16	13-13	**Qemah** D, BF	3 9-0	127^{-4}	6-1	Jean-Claude Rouget (FR)	won Prix de la Grotte Gp3 (1m) (1)
15	32-11	**Ervedya** D	3 9-0	129^{-1}	3-1	Jean-Claude Rouget (FR)	won Prix Imprudence Gp3 (7f) (1)
14	312-7	**Rizeena** C	3 9-0	127^T	11-2	Clive Brittain	won Moyglare Stud Stakes Gp1 (7f) (2)

FAVOURITES -£0.32

TRAINERS IN THIS RACE (w-pl-r) Jessica Harrington 2-1-4, Jean-Claude Rouget 2-1-3, Aidan O'Brien 1-5-16, Andrew Balding 1-0-3, Francis Graffard 1-0-1, John & Thady Gosden 1-0-3, Dermot Weld 1-0-2, Richard Hannon 0-1-6, Ralph Beckett 0-1-3

FATE OF FAVOURITES 0261123511 **POSITION OF WINNER IN MARKET** 3241173311

THIS prestigious and valuable 1m4f handicap for three-year-olds and upwards dates back to 1914 and was formerly known as the Bessborough Handicap (starting out as a sprint) before being renamed in 1999.

Last year's winner Okita Soushi, third in the Copper Horse Handicap over 1m6f in 2022, dropped back to this trip to score by a neck at 9-1 for Joseph O'Brien.

Form An official rating in the mid-to-high 90s is typical of most runners, and therefore winners, nowadays. To achieve that, most will have been running in Class 2 or 3 handicaps at the better tracks. Six of the last ten winners had won last time out.

Draw Okita Soushi came out of stall nine last year, ending a run of 14

Key trends
▶ *Achieved best RPR in a Class 2 or 3 handicap, 10/10*
▶ *Drawn in double figures, 9/10*
▶ *Aged four or five, 9/10*
▶ *Top-three finish last time, 7/10 (six won)*
▶ *Officially rated between 96 and 102, 7/10*

Other factors
▶ *Five of the last ten winners started favourite, including one joint-favourite*

consecutive winners drawn in double figures. The next four came from stalls 11 to 19 (the highest), while the unplaced favourite was in six.

Key races The 1m4f handicaps at Newmarket's Guineas meeting, York's Dante fixture and the Epsom Derby meeting often provide good guides. Between Okita Soushi and the previous

Irish-trained winner (Katiykha in 2000), 14 of the 22 winners had form at one of those meetings and 12 of those had achieved a top-six placing (though only five won). A good run at the Goodwood trials fixture in mid-May is also worth noting, while four of the last nine winners had run at Royal Ascot the previous year (finishing 8513).

Trainers Remarkably, Sir Michael Stoute, Mark Johnston (whose yard has now passed to son Charlie) and Hughie Morrison have had 13 of the last 25 winners between them.

Betting There have been six successful favourites (outright or joint) in the last 13 runnings after a long gap back to the Queen's Blueprint in 1999. The winner has been 10-1 or bigger in ten of the 24 runnings since Blueprint.

Story of the last ten years

	FORM	WINNER	AGE & WGT	OR	SP	TRAINER	BEST RPR LAST 12 MONTHS (RUNS SINCE)
23	0-115	**Okita Soushi** D	5 9-9	102-3	9-1	Joseph O'Brien (IRE)	5th Saval Beg Stakes Gp3 (1m6f) (0)
22	2d331-	**Candleford** D	4 8-12	91-5	11-2	William Haggas	won Kempton Class 2 hcap (1m4f) (0)
21	6/13-1	**Quickthorn** D	4 9-3	97-6	7-2f	Hughie Morrison	won Haydock Class 3 hcap (1m4f) (0)
20	034-5	**Scarlet Dragon** D	7 9-2	97-2	33-1	Alan King	4th Goodwood Class 2 hcap (1m6f) (4)
19	11-31	**Baghdad** CD	4 9-8	104-1	7-2f	Mark Johnston	won Newmarket Class 2 hcap (1m4f) (0)
18	1-221	**Dash Of Spice** D	4 9-3	98T	7-2f	David Elsworth	won Epsom Class 2 hcap (1m4f) (0)
17	171/8-	**Rare Rhythm** D	5 9-2	97-4	20-1	Charlie Appleby	Seasonal debut (0)
16	22-01	**Kinema**	5 9-4	99-3	8-1	Ralph Beckett	won Goodwood Class 2 hcap (1m6f) (0)
15	342-3	**Arab Dawn** BF	4 9-2	96T	6-1j	Hughie Morrison	3rd Newmarket Class 2 hcap (1m4f) (0)
14	2-111	**Arab Spring** D	4 9-10	104-3	11-4f	Sir Michael Stoute	won York Class 2 hcap (1m4f) (0)

WINS-PL-RUNS 4yo 6-12-84, 5yo 3-10-48, 6yo+ 1-8-41 **FAVOURITES** £10.75

FATE OF FAVOURITES 1120113180 **POSITION OF WINNER IN MARKET** 1148110136

NTRODUCED to the Royal Ascot programme in 2002, this is a handicap for three-year-old fillies rated 0-105 run over the straight mile, making it effectively a fillies' version of the Britannia.

Last year's winner

Coppice was typically unexposed for John and Thady Gosden, having won her only start at two, finished down the field in the Group 3 Nell Gwyn on her reappearance and then won a mile novice on the Newcastle all-weather.

Form

Fourteen of the 22 winners had already tasted success that season (ten were last-time-out winners) and three in the past decade went to Royal Ascot unbeaten in three previous starts.

Draw

Racing on one of the two wings tends to be an advantage. Eight of the last ten winners were drawn in the six highest or five lowest stalls. Coppice last year came out of stall 25 (seventh highest in the field of 29).

Key races

A good test is important in preparation for this fast-paced race, either in Group/Listed company or a decent-sized field in a handicap. Twelve of the 22 winners had already won over a mile or further.

Trainers

The Gosden stable (Persuasive in 2016 and Coppice), Richard Hannon (Osaila in 2015 and Heredia in 2022) and Charlie Fellowes (Thanks Be in 2019 and Onassis in 2020) have all struck twice in the past nine runnings.

Betting

Despite the race's large number of runners and hugely competitive nature, it is notable that fancied contenders do well. Twelve of the 22 winners came from the top two in the betting, including eight who had at least a share of favouritism, and only five winners have been bigger than 11-1 (although two of the last five were 33-1).

Key trends

▶ *Lost maiden tag, 9/10*
▶ *Drawn in the six highest or the five lowest stalls, 8/10*
▶ *Carried no more than 9st 3lb, 7/10*
▶ *Won over 7f or a mile earlier that season, 7/10*
▶ *No more than three juvenile starts, 7/10*

Other factors

▶ *Five winners ran in handicaps as three-year-olds (four won at least one; exception finished second)*
▶ *Four winners had contested a Listed or Group race at three*

Story of the last ten years

	FORM	WINNER	AGE	& WGT	OR	SP	TRAINER	BEST RPR LAST 12 MONTHS (RUNS SINCE)
23	1-01	**Coppice** D	3	9-3	97-10	6-1j	John & Thady Gosden	won Newcastle Class 5 novice (1m) (0)
22	11-1	**Heredia**	3	9-8	98T	7-2f	Richard Hannon	won York Class 3 handicap (7f) (0)
21	3-101	**Create Belief** D	3	9-2	97T	6-1	Johnny Murtagh (IRE)	won Curragh handicap (1m) (0)
20	7251-	**Onassis**	3	8-1	81-14	33-1	Charlie Fellowes	won Newcastle Class 4 handicap (7f) (0)
19	55-22	**Thanks Be** (4oh)	3	8-0	84-6	33-1	Charlie Fellowes	2nd Nottingham Class 4 hcp (1m2f) (0)
18	6-21	**Agrotera** D	3	8-7	88-5	11-2f	Ed Walker	2nd Ascot Class 3 conditions (1m) (1)
17	142-4	**Con Te Partiro**	3	9-5	102-12	20-1	Wesley Ward (USA)	4th Belmont Park Listed (7f) (0)
16	1-11	**Persuasive**	3	8-9	95T	11-4f	John Gosden	won Chelmsford Class 2 hcp (1m) (0)
15	13-17	**Osaila** CD	3	9-7	107-3	13-2	Richard Hannon	5th Moyglare Stud Stakes Gp1 (7f) (4)
14	1-11	**Muteela**	3	8-13	95T	9-2f	Mark Johnston	won Newmarket Class3 hcap (1m) (0)

FAVOURITES £13.75

FATE OF FAVOURITES 121010P211 **POSITION OF WINNER IN MARKET** 1219109211

Horseboxes - Uprating and Downplating

Uprating Horseboxes

As you may be aware, the DVSA is paying close attention to the horsebox industry and in particular, to lightweight horseboxes which they suspect may be operating overweight.

We have seen cases of horseboxes being stopped, checked and impounded on the roadside, owing to running overweight. The horses in transit have to be loaded into a different box and taken away, and the resultant fines are ever increasing in size. Yet, there is an alternative.

SvTech is keen to promote its uprating service for lightweight horseboxes (3500kg), whereby the horsebox can gain an extra 200-300kg in payload. This provides vital payload capability when carrying an extra horse and/ or tack and offers peace of mind for the owner.

SvTech has carried out extensive work and testing on lightweight models and has covered uprates for most lightweight vehicles.

It is worth noting that some uprates require modifications or changes to the vehicle's braking, tyres and/or suspension, for which SvTech provides a simple purpose-built suspension assister kit. This will take between 1-2 hours for you to fit. Your horsebox will then go for a formal inspection to bring it into the 'Goods' category, and, depending on the vehicle's age, may also require fitment of a speed limiter, for which there are one or two options. Most importantly, vehicles registered after May 2002 must be fitted with manufacturer's ABS, if going above 3500kg.

If you're unsure, or don't believe that you need to uprate your lightweight horsebox, try taking it to a public weighbridge when you're fully loaded with your horse, tack, passenger, hay, etc. and weigh off each axle individually and the vehicle as a whole. There could be a distinct chance that you've overloaded one of the axles, even if you're within the GVW. If there is a problem, we can help. Call us to discuss your options.

Downplating Horseboxes

Do you own a 10 - 12.5 tonnes horsebox and do you want non-HGV licence holder to drive it? Your horsebox could be downplated to 7.5 tonnes so that any driver with a licence issued prior to 1st Jan 1997 could drive it.

- You are paying too much Vehicle Excise Duty.
- You want to escape the need for a tachograph.

The most important aspect when downplating is to leave yourself suitable payload to carry your goods. The Ministry requires that for horseboxes of 7500kg there is a minimum payload of 2000kg. Hence, when downplating to 7500kg, the unladen weight must not exceed 5500kg. For 3500kg horseboxes, you must ensure that you have a payload of at least 1000kg, thus, when empty it cannot weigh more than 2500kg.

Due to recent changes at DVSA, we are no longer required to make a mechanical change to the vehicle and, once downrated, we will be supplying you with a revised set of Ministry plating certificates, or if exempt, plating and testing, a converter's plate and certificate at the lower weight.

Depending upon vehicle usage, it is at the discretion of DVSA as to whether they will require a formal inspection of your vehicle.

TO DISCOVER YOUR OPTIONS, PLEASE DOWNLOAD, FILL IN AND RETURN OUR ENQUIRY FORM – WWW.SVTECH.CO.UK

SvTech
Special Vehicle Technology

T +44 (0)1772 621800
E webenquiries@svtech.co.uk

DATING back to 1834, this Group 2 over 1m4f for three-year-olds comes just under three weeks after the Derby at Epsom and was once officially called the Ascot Derby, as it still is colloquially, such is the close link between the races.

Last year's winner King Of Steel came here after his half-length second to Auguste Rodin in the Derby and clearly was the class act as 11-10 favourite in a field of six, fitting nearly every key trend and scoring easily by three and a half lengths.

Form King Of Steel had been more highly tried at two than most winners, having gone straight from a maiden win to the Group 1 Futurity, although he disappointed in seventh. The norm is to improve at three

Key trends

▸ *Won within last three starts, 10/10*
▸ *Adjusted RPR of at least 120, 8/10*
▸ *Yet to win over 1m4f, 8/10*
▸ *Within 5lb of RPR top-rated, 9/10 (five were top-rated)*
▸ *Ran in a recognised Derby trial, 8/10 (four won)*
▸ *Top-three finish last time out, 6/10*

Other factors

▸ *Three of the last five winners had run in Group company as juveniles – Japan, Pyledriver and King Of Steel (Japan won a Group 2)*

to go on the Classic trail – and that was a pattern followed by King Of Steel,

whose RPR of 96 at two was up to 122 by the time he arrived at Royal Ascot.

Key races Many King Edward VII winners have graduated from the Derby, including five of the last seven under the normal schedule (not including the lockdown year of 2020 when the races were the other way round).

Trainers Sir Michael Stoute has won the race seven times. The stables built up by Mark Johnston and John Gosden have had three winners apiece. Aidan O'Brien (also three in total) has had two winners and four runners-up in the past decade.

Betting Seven of the last ten winners came from the top three in the betting and 20 of the last 25 winners have been no bigger than 7-1.

Story of the last ten years

	FORM	WINNER	AGE & WGT	Adj RPR	SP	TRAINER	BEST RPR LAST 12 MONTHS (RUNS SINCE)
23	17-2	**King Of Steel**	3 9-2	134^T	11-10f	Roger Varian	2nd Derby Gp1 (1m4f) (0)
22	2-115	**Changingoftheguard** D 3 9-2		126^T	11-10f	Aidan O'Brien (IRE)	won Chester Vase Gp3 (1m4½f) (1)
21	12-1	**Alenquer**	3 9-0	123^T	13-8f	William Haggas	won Sandown Classic Trial Gp3 (1m2f) (0)
20	417-2	**Pyledriver**	3 9-0	118^{-5}	18-1	William Muir	2nd Classic Trial Gp3 (1m2f) (0)
19	11-43	**Japan**	3 9-0	132^T	6-4f	Aidan O'Brien (IRE)	3rd Derby Gp1 (1m4f) (0)
18	7-121	**Old Persian**	3 9-0	120^{-4}	9-2	Charlie Appleby	won Newmarket Listed (1m2f) (0)
17	32110	**Permian**	3 9-0	128^T	6-1	Mark Johnston	won Dante Stakes Gp2 (1m2½f) (1)
16	2-130	**Across The Stars** D	3 9-0	120^{-2}	7-1	Sir Michael Stoute	3rd Lingfield Derby Trial Listed (1m3½f) (1)
15	1-2	**Balios**	3 9-0	123^{-5}	3-1	David Simcock	2nd Newmarket Stakes Listed (1m2f) (0)
14	14	**Eagle Top** BF	3 9-0	114^{-10}	12-1	John Gosden	4th Leicester Class 3 hcap (1m4f) (0)

FAVOURITES -£0.68

TRAINERS IN THIS RACE (w-pl-r) Aidan O'Brien 2-6-16, William Haggas 1-0-5, Charlie Appleby 1-0-4, Roger Varian 1-0-3, Andrew Balding 0-2-4, John & Thady Gosden 0-0-1, Ralph Beckett 0-0-4, James Fanshawe 0-0-1, Richard Hannon 0-0-2

FATE OF FAVOURITES 2P23514111 **POSITION OF WINNER IN MARKET** 6242315111

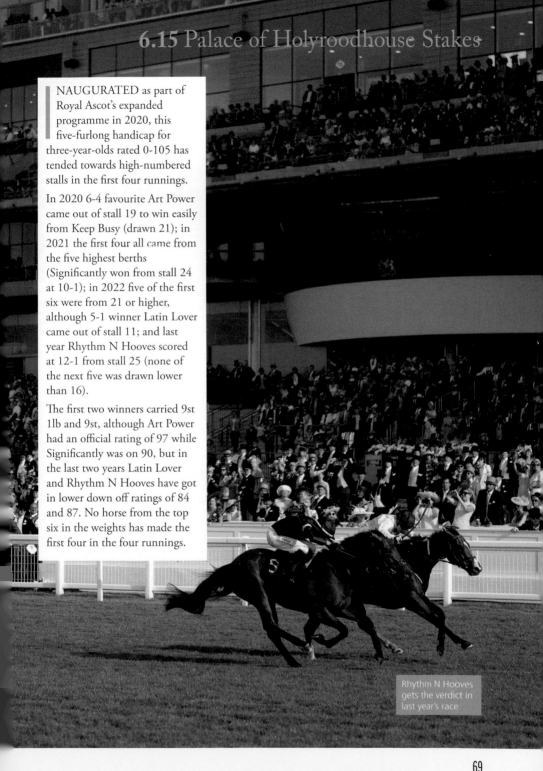

NAUGURATED as part of Royal Ascot's expanded programme in 2020, this five-furlong handicap for three-year-olds rated 0-105 has tended towards high-numbered stalls in the first four runnings.

In 2020 6-4 favourite Art Power came out of stall 19 to win easily from Keep Busy (drawn 21); in 2021 the first four all came from the five highest berths (Significantly won from stall 24 at 10-1); in 2022 five of the first six were from 21 or higher, although 5-1 winner Latin Lover came out of stall 11; and last year Rhythm N Hooves scored at 12-1 from stall 25 (none of the next five was drawn lower than 16).

The first two winners carried 9st 1lb and 9st, although Art Power had an official rating of 97 while Significantly was on 90, but in the last two years Latin Lover and Rhythm N Hooves have got in lower down off ratings of 84 and 87. No horse from the top six in the weights has made the first four in the four runnings.

Rhythm N Hooves gets the verdict in last year's race

EXPERT VIEW

Racing Post analysts Mark Brown and Richard Young pick a dozen contenders who have signalled winning potential

ALMAQAM

3yo colt
Trainer: Ed Walker

Almaqam is a three-year-old of considerable potential, highly regarded by his trainer, and has multiple options at the royal meeting.

The son of Lope De Vega returned with a likeable win in a mile maiden at Yarmouth in April and ought to relish a step up to 1m2f.

The Group 3 Hampton Court Stakes, won by his trainer last season with Waipiro, looks a natural target, for all that improvement is needed, and if his prep run doesn't work out then he could easily take the handicap route and go for the Golden Gates. (MB)

CAMILLE PISSARRO

2yo colt
Aidan O'Brien

Aidan O'Brien has won the Coventry Stakes ten times, including last year with River Tiber, and Camille Pissarro took the same Navan 6f maiden that one did on his debut in April.

A 1,250,000gns son of Wootton Bassett, Camille Pissarro pulled clear late without Ryan Moore having to get serious on that first start. He's bred for the job as a half-brother to Golden Horde, who was fifth in the 2019 Coventry before winning the Commonwealth Cup a year later. (MB)

COURAGE MON AMI

5yo gelding
John & Thady Gosden

Courage Mon Ami has prospects of becoming the fourth this century to win the Ascot Gold Cup more than once.

The John and Thady Gosden-trained five-year-old stepped up considerably on previous form to win the race last year on only his fourth start.

He wasn't at his best in the Goodwood Cup but returned to form back on a sound surface in the Lonsdale Cup at York on his final start of 2023.

The return to 2m4f will suit and he can provide owner Wathnan Racing's retained jockey James Doyle with his second win in the race. (RY)

Eyecatchers

Attention grabbers: Courage Mon Ami and (below) Gallantly

DESERT HERO

4yo gelding
William Haggas

Desert Hero can notch a second successive Royal Ascot win by taking the Group 2 Hardwicke Stakes over 1m4f.

Owned by King Charles and Queen Camilla, the four-year-old has come a fair way since winning the King George V Handicap at this meeting last year.

He ran as though retaining his ability on his reappearance. Although he disappointed at Newbury on Lockinge day, he was a bit keen in the first half of the contest and didn't get much room at a crucial stage. His overall record suggests he's worth another chance. (RY)

GALLANTLY

3yo colt Aidan O'Brien

This son of Frankel took four attempts to get off the mark, but as expected showed a marked improvement in form upped to 1m2½f on good ground at Chester's May meeting, comfortably accounting for a useful yardstick.

As with many from the yard, Gallantly is the type to keep progressing, especially as he goes up to 1m4f, with the King George V Handicap looking an ideal target.

Interestingly, Secret State won the same Chester maiden before following up in that Royal Ascot handicap in 2022. (MB)

71

EXPERT VIEW

LONDON CITY

3yo colt
Aidan O'Brien

Aidan O'Brien needs one more win in the Queen's Vase to draw level with Sir Henry Cecil on eight and looks to have solid claims with London City.

The blue-blooded colt – by US Triple Crown winner Justify out of multiple Group 1 scorer Winter – turned in his best effort upped to 1m4f when winning on his handicap debut at York in May, his first run on a sound surface.

The way he saw out his race suggests he'll be at least as good over 1m6f at Royal Ascot and there's almost certainly more improvement in him. (RY)

PASSENGER

4yo colt
Sir Michael Stoute

Judging by his May win at Chester, Sir Michael Stoute's Passenger is going to be a leading player in the top 1m2f events this season.

The four-year-old stepped up on previous efforts to beat a good yardstick in Israr in the Huxley Stakes, shaving nearly two seconds off the Chester track record.

The manner of the win was impressive and he can make his mark back in Group 1 company. (RY)

REAL DREAM

5yo gelding
Sir Michael Stoute

This one looks a typical slow-burner from the Stoute yard and should be ready to step up on his Newmarket reappearance, which came over an inadequate 1m4f.

The Copper Horse Handicap over 1m6f looks the ideal target for the son of Lope De Vega, who was an impressive winner over the same course and distance last summer.

There still looks some room for manoeuvre in his mark of 102 and it would be no surprise if he progressed to Listed/Group 3 races later in the season. (MB)

Real Dream: right type for the Copper Horse Handicap

Eyecatchers

Treasure (left): Ribblesdale looks an obvious target for the royal runner

ROHAAN

6yo gelding
David Evans

It's doubtful any horse in training has a better Ascot record than Rohaan. The David Evans-trained sprinter has won half of his ten starts at the track, including the Wokingham in 2021 and 2022.

A tilt at a Group 1 event at last year's meeting proved unproductive but he came good back at Ascot in a handicap last October.

He's shown he retains a good chunk of ability this season and the Wokingham, rather than the Group route, looks the way to go this time. (RY)

ROSALLION

3yo colt
Richard Hannon

Richard Hannon has long been clear in his high regard for Rosallion and the son of Blue Point, having signed off his juvenile campaign with an impressive win in the Group 1 Prix Jean-Luc Lagardere, moved through the 2,000 Guineas like the equal of race-fit winner Notable Speech.

Following that sterling second, the St James's Palace Stakes looks tailor-made for him around a bend, providing the ground isn't testing. (MB)

TREASURE

3yo filly
Ralph Beckett

Ralph Beckett is often well represented in the middle-distance three-year-old division and this year has been no different, including victories in the Cheshire Oaks and Lingfield Oaks Trial.

Treasure ran in the latter contest, finishing fourth behind stablemate You Got To Me and shaping as if in need of the run on ground that would have been plenty fast enough.

The big, scopey daughter of Mastercraftsman is open to plenty of improvement and, being owned by the King and Queen, the Ribblesdale Stakes at the royal meeting is an obvious target. (MB)

VANDEEK

3yo colt
Simon & Ed Crisford

When you've got so much speed, why try to stretch it out to the Classic distances of at least a mile?

The decision to sidestep the 2,000 Guineas could prove smart with the Simon and Ed Crisford-trained Vandeek, who reserved his best efforts for Group 1 events at two, winning the Prix Morny at Deauville and the Middle Park at Newmarket.

He's reportedly done well over the winter, goes on any ground and has to be a strong fancy in the Commonwealth Cup. (RY)

DAY FIVE

The Queen Elizabeth II Jubilee Stakes takes top billing as the final Group 1 of the week on a card that features everything from top sprinters to out-and-out stayers.

A reshuffle sees the Hardwicke Stakes move up from fourth to second on the bill, swapping places with the Jersey Stakes.

Sandwiched between them is the Queen Elizabeth II Jubilee, a six-furlong contest for older horses that has a reputation for attracting the best sprinters from all parts of the globe, with winners from Australia, Hong Kong and the United States in recent years. Last year's race produced a huge shock with Khaadem's 80-1 victory.

The Group 2 on the card is the Hardwicke, a long-established Royal Ascot favourite and regularly a pointer to the King George VI and Queen Elizabeth Stakes at the royal track in July. Last year's race went to the popular Pyledriver, the previous season's King George winner.

The other Group race is the Jersey, a Group 3 over seven furlongs that can be a proving ground for a star three-year-old in the making.

The two-year-olds open the card in the seven-furlong Chesham Stakes, which attracts those who are likely to excel at a mile or further during their three-year-old careers. Classic winners Churchill and Masar both competed in this race in recent years.

The last heritage handicap of the week is the Wokingham Stakes over six furlongs, which brings together a big field of up to 30 runners and a competitive betting market. That is followed by the Golden Gates Stakes, a mile-and-a-quarter handicap for three-year-olds that joined the bill in 2020.

The royal meeting closes with the Queen Alexandra Stakes, the much-loved test over two and three-quarter miles that provides the traditional ending to the five-day meeting.

Saturday June 22

2.30 **Chesham Stakes** (Listed) **7f** Last year's winner: Snellen 12-1	2yo	£110,000
3.05 **Hardwicke Stakes** (Group 2) **1m4f** Last year's winner: Pyledriver 7-2	4yo+	£250,000
3.45 **Queen Elizabeth II Jubilee Stakes** (Group 1) **6f** Last year's winner: Khaadem 80-1	4yo+	£1,000,000
4.25 **Jersey Stakes** (Group 3) **7f** Last year's winner: Age Of Kings 22-1	3yo	£150,000
5.05 **Wokingham Stakes** (Heritage Handicap) **6f** Last year's winner: Saint Lawrence 22-1	3yo+	£175,000
5.40 **Golden Gates Stakes** (Handicap) **1m2f** Last year's winner: Burdett Road 20-1	3yo	£110,000
6.15 **Queen Alexandra Stakes** (Conditions) **2m6f** Last year's winner: Dawn Rising 2-1f	4yo+	£110,000 Race value is total prize-money

FIRST run in 1919, this Listed contest is the final race of the meeting for two-year-olds and at seven furlongs is the longest of the week for that age group. It is designed to provide an early stamina test for youngsters, being open only to horses whose sire or dam won over a distance in excess of nine and a half furlongs.

Last year's winner

Snellen became a second juvenile filly success at Royal Ascot for County Meath trainer Gavin Cromwell, better known for his jumps exploits, when she stepped up from her Limerick maiden debut win just ten days earlier to strike at 12-1.

Form Since the race distance was raised to seven furlongs in 1996, most of the 28 winners had raced only once,

Key trends

▶ *Rated within 9lb of RPR top-rated, eight winners in last ten runnings*
▶ *Raced just once, 8/10 (five had won)*
▶ *By a sire with a stamina index of at least 8.7f, 7/10*
▶ *Recorded Topspeed figure of at least 63, 6/10*
▶ *Adjusted RPR of at least 91, 7/10*

Other factors

▶ *Since Bach in 1999, only three winners had previously scored over 7f – September in 2017, Point Lonsdale in 2021 (both trained by Aidan O'Brien) and last year's winner Snellen*
▶ *The record of fillies is 2-30*

with 19 having won (15 had won their sole start).

Key races Seven of the last ten winners had made their debut less than four weeks before this race (and 2022 winner Holloway Boy hadn't run at all). Only three had run over 7f. Curragh, Newbury and Newmarket maidens are often an indicator of high regard.

Trainers Aidan O'Brien – the dominant force in Classics both at a mile and over middle distances – has won four times in the last eight years. Also keep a close eye on John and Thady Gosden and Godolphin trainers Charlie Appleby and Saeed bin Suroor.

Betting Nine of the 28 winners since 1996 had market leadership, with a further 13 in the top four in the betting.

Story of the last ten years

	FORM	WINNER	AGE & WGT	Adj RPR	SP	TRAINER	BEST RPR LAST 12 MONTHS (RUNS SINCE)
23	1	**Snellen** D	2 9-0	96·8	16-1	Gavin Cromwell (IRE)	won Limerick maiden (7f) (0)
22		**Holloway Boy**	2 9-5	0	40-1	Karl Burke	Debutant
21	1	**Point Lonsdale** D	2 9-3	106T	10-11f	Aidan O'Brien (IRE)	won Curragh maiden (7f) (0)
20	5	**Battleground**	2 9-3	90·6	11-4f	Aidan O'Brien (IRE)	5th Naas maiden (6f) (0)
19	11	**Pinatubo**	2 9-3	107T	3-1	Charlie Appleby	won Epsom Class 2 conditions (6f) (0)
18	1	**Arthur Kitt**	2 9-3	100·9	13-2	Tom Dascombe	won Haydock Class 4 novice (6f) (0)
17	1	**September** D	2 8-12	107T	11-8f	Aidan O'Brien (IRE)	won Leopardstown maiden (7f) (0)
16	3	**Churchill** BF	2 9-3	95·9	8-11f	Aidan O'Brien (IRE)	3rd Curragh maiden (6f) (0)
15	1	**Sunny Way**	2 9-3	91·7	14-1	Eoghan O'Neill (FR)	won Maisons-Laffitte maiden (6f) (0)
14	4	**Richard Pankhurst** BF	2 9-3	87·23	10-1	John Gosden	4th Newmarket Class 4 maiden (6f) (0)

FAVOURITES £-0.24

TRAINERS IN THIS RACE (w-pl-r) Aidan O'Brien 4-4-14, Charlie Appleby 1-1-6, Karl Burke 1-0-2, Richard Hannon 0-0-8, Andrew Balding 0-1-6, John & Thady Gosden 0-1-4, Paul & Oliver Cole 0-0-1, Roger Varian 0-0-1, Ralph Beckett 0-0-1

FATE OF FAVOURITES 3211021162 **POSITION OF WINNER IN MARKET** 4611321105

FIRST run in 1879, this Group 2 race over 1m4f is for four-year-olds and upwards and often provides a showcase for horses who were in the Derby picture the previous year.

Last year's winner

Pyledriver became the second consecutive six-year-old winner after Broome in 2022 (the last before them had been in 2007). Apart from age, he ticked all the main boxes having established his class with Group 1 wins in the 2021 Coronation Cup and 2022 King George and his course-and-distance victory in the King Edward VII Stakes at the 2020 royal meeting.

Form

An adjusted RPR of 128 has been the minimum standard required since 2010 and most winners have been in the 130s, which points to a Group 1 performer. Five of the last ten winners had run in a Group 1 last time and three of the others were coming off victory in a lower-level Group race.

Key trends

▶ *Group-race winner, 10/10*
▶ *Adjusted RPR of at least 128, 10/10*
▶ *Rated within 8lb of RPR top-rated, 10/10*
▶ *Distance winner, 9/10*
▶ *Top-two finish last time out, 8/10*
▶ *Aged four, 7/10*
▶ *Finished in the first three in a Listed or Group race that season, 7/10*

Other factors

▶ *Six winners scored last time out*
▶ *Four winners were RPR top-rated*

Key races

All but three of the last 16 winners were aged four and many had followed similar career paths to this point, with nine of them having competed the previous year in at least one of the St Leger, the Great Voltigeur Stakes at York or the King Edward VII at Royal Ascot.

Trainers

This is Sir Michael Stoute's best race at Royal Ascot with 11 winners, eight of them in the last 18 runnings, and Aidan O'Brien has had four winners, all since 2008.

Betting

The market has been an excellent guide recently, with 14 of the last 18 winners coming from the first three in the betting. Six of the seven successful favourites in that period were trained by Stoute or O'Brien.

Story of the last ten years

	FORM	WINNER	AGE & WGT	Adj RPR	SP	TRAINER	BEST RPR LAST 12 MONTHS (RUNS SINCE)
23	0421-	**Pyledriver** CD	6 9-3	136ᵀ	7-2	W Muir & C Grassick	won King George Gp1 (1m4f) (0)
22	020-5	**Broome** D	6 9-3	132⁻⁴	6-1	Aidan O'Brien (IRE)	2nd Breeders' Cup Turf Gp1 (1m4f) (1)
21	1511-	**Wonderful Tonight** CD	4 8-12	135⁻¹	5-1	David Menuisier	won Fillies & Mares Gp1 (1m4f) (0)
20	114-2	**Fanny Logan** BF	4 8-12	128⁻⁷	17-2	John Gosden	2nd Haydock Gp3 (1m3½f) (0)
19	2-421	**Defoe** D	5 9-1	135ᵀ	11-4f	Roger Varian	won Coronation Cup Gp1 (1m4f) (0)
18	12-11	**Crystal Ocean** D	4 9-1	135ᵀ	4-7f	Sir Michael Stoute	won Aston Park Stakes Gp3 (1m4f) (0)
17	1U5-6	**Idaho** D	4 9-1	133⁻¹	9-2	Aidan O'Brien (IRE)	2nd Irish Derby Gp1 (1m4f) (4)
16	53-11	**Dartmouth** CD	4 9-1	129⁻⁷	10-1	Sir Michael Stoute	won Ormonde Stakes Gp3 (1m5½f) (0)
15	237-1	**Snow Sky** D	4 9-1	130⁻⁸	12-1	Sir Michael Stoute	won Yorkshire Cup Gp2 (1m6f) (0)
14	21-22	**Telescope** D	4 9-1	130ᵀ	7-4f	Sir Michael Stoute	2nd Huxley Stakes Gp3 (1m2½f) (0)

WINS-RUNS 4yo 7-8-42, 5yo 1-7-23, 6yo+ 2-1-19 **FAVOURITES** -£1.93

TRAINERS IN THIS RACE (w-pl-r) Sir Michael Stoute 4-2-13, Aidan O'Brien 2-2-11, John & Thady Gosden 0-1-2, Owen Burrows 0-1-1, Andrew Balding 0-1-3, Charlie Appleby 0-0-2, William Haggas 0-0-3, Ralph Beckett 0-1-3, Willie Mullins 0-0-1

FATE OF FAVOURITES 1604115235 **POSITION OF WINNER IN MARKET** 1462116332

DAY FIVE

NAUGURATED in 1868 and long known as the Cork and Orrery Stakes, this has held Group 1 status since 2002 when it was renamed first to celebrate the golden jubilee of Queen Elizabeth II. This is the big 6f sprint of the week for older horses (open only to four-year-olds and upwards since the advent of the Commonwealth Cup for three-year-olds).

Last year's winner

Khaadem scored a huge upset at 80-1, doubling the post-war record odds in this race. The Charlie Hills-trained seven-year-old was a trends-buster on age and ratings, although in his younger days he had been beaten less than two lengths in fourth as a 13-2 shot in the 2020 race.

Form Most winners bring a strong level of form, with 17 out of 22 since the upgrade to Group 1 having been placed at least in this grade in the previous 12 months (11 had won). The other five had at least competed at that level. Khaadem had been fourth in the Group 1 Nunthorpe at York the previous summer.

Key races The British Champions Sprint, run over course and distance the previous October, is a key guide. Five of the last nine British or Irish winners had run there, finishing 12188,

with the exceptions being 2018 winner Merchant Navy, who was trained by Aidan O'Brien but had arrived only recently from Australia; Godolphin's Blue Point and Naval Crown, who had been sent to Dubai for the winter; and Khaadem.

The best prep race has been the Duke of York Stakes, with five of the 15 British-trained winners since 2002 having run there for finishing positions of 03255 (O'Brien's Starspangledbanner also prepped there in 2010, finishing fifth).

One explanation for the step up in performance from the Duke of York (and the fact that only seven of the last 22 winners had scored on their previous outing) is that the

ground often changes from softish in May to much faster in June.

Sixteen of the last 22 runnings have been contested on good to firm (or firm) and 13 of the 16 winners in those years had already won on that kind of surface.

The main races to check for the type who has been placed in a Group 1 but not yet won at that level are the previous year's running of this race, the July Cup and Haydock Sprint Cup.

Trainers Charlie Appleby is the only trainer with more than one win in the past ten runnings, having scored with Blue Point (also a dual winner of the King's Stand

3.45 Queen Elizabeth II Jubilee Stakes

Charlie Hills with Khaadem, last year's 80-1 winner

Stakes) in 2019 and Naval Crown in 2022.

Betting Since the race was upgraded to Group 1, ten of the 22 winners were priced in double figures, with only five successful favourites.

Roll of honour

Longest-priced winner
80-1 Khaadem (2023)

Shortest-priced winner
1-6 Black Caviar (2012)

Most successful trainer
5 wins: **Vincent O'Brien**
Welsh Saint (1970), Saritamer (1974), Swingtime (1975), Thatching (1979), College Chapel (1993)

Most successful jockey
9 wins: **Lester Piggott**
Right Boy (1958, 1959), Tin Whistle (1960), El Gallo (1963), Mountain Call (1968), Welsh Saint (1970), Saritamer (1974), Thatching (1979), College Chapel (1993)

Most successful owner
3 wins: **Godolphin**
So Factual (1995), Blue Point (2019), Naval Crown (2022)

*All figures since 1946

Key trends

▶ Top-three finish within last two starts, 9/10
▶ Group or Listed winner over 6f, 9/10
▶ Adjusted RPR of at least 127, 8/10 (last two winners the exceptions)
▶ Rated within 8lb of RPR top-rated, 8/10
▶ No older than five, 8/10

Other factors

▶ Five winners had yet to score that season
▶ Three winners had run in the race the year before, finishing 782, while seven winners had contested a previous Royal Ascot (one won, three placed and three unplaced)

Story of the last ten years

	FORM	WINNER	AGE & WGT	Adj RPR	SP	TRAINER	BEST RPR LAST 12 MONTHS (RUNS SINCE)
23	-0603	**Khaadem** D	7 9-5	123-11	80-1	Charlie Hills	won King George Stakes Gp2 (5f) (6)
22	8-104	**Naval Crown** D	4 9-5	123-11	33-1	Charlie Appleby	4th Al Quoz Sprint Gp1 (6f) (0)
21	118-1	**Dream Of Dreams** D	7 9-3	134T	3-1f	Sir Michael Stoute	won Windsor Listed (6f) (0)
20	1318-	**Hello Youmzain** D	4 9-3	132T	4-1	Kevin Ryan	won Haydock Sprint Cup Gp1 (6f) (1)
19	-1111	**Blue Point** CD	5 9-3	137T	6-4f	Charlie Appleby	won King's Stand Stakes Gp1 (5f) (0)
18	1-331	**Merchant Navy** D	4 9-3	131-8	4-1	Aidan O'Brien (IRE)	won Greenlands Stakes Gp2 (6f) (0)
17	121-5	**The Tin Man** CD	5 9-3	132-5	9-2	James Fanshawe	won Champions Sprint Gp1 (6f) (1)
16	112-5	**Twilight Son** D	4 9 3	132T	7-2	Henry Candy	2nd Champions Sprint Gp1 (6f) (1)
15	33-32	**Undrafted** D	5 9-3	127-8	14-1	Wesley Ward (USA)	3rd Breeders' Cup Turf Sprint Gd1 (6½f) (2)
14	210-1	**Slade Power** CD	5 9-4	131T	7-2f	Eddie Lynam (IRE)	won Greenlands Stakes Gp3 (6f) (0)

WINS-RUNS 3yo 0-1-2, 4yo 4-10-62, 5yo 4-5-43, 6yo+ 2-5-41 **FAVOURITES** £1.00

TRAINERS IN THIS RACE (w-pl-r) Charlie Appleby 2-1-6, Aidan O'Brien 1-1-7, Charlie Hills 1-0-7, Kevin Ryan 1-1-5, Henry Candy 1-1-6, Roger Varian 0-1-2, Andrew Balding 0-0-6, Clive Cox 0-0-3, William Haggas 0-2-5, Archie Watson 0-1-1, Ralph Beckett 0-0-2

FATE OF FAVOURITES 1243013103 **POSITION OF WINNER IN MARKET** 1632212100

DATING back to 1919, this Group 3 race for three-year-olds over seven furlongs is a battleground between Classic pretenders dropping back from a mile and sprinters trying to stretch out their stamina.

Last year's winner Age Of Kings was sent off at 22-1 for Aidan O'Brien, which reflected his patchy record on the track and on key trends. However, he was highly regarded enough to have run in the Coventry (seventh) at two and the Irish 2,000 Guineas (tenth) on his reappearance at three and scored by a length from Zoology (also 22-1) and Streets Of Gold (28-1).

Form Most winners had been highly tried already and

Key trends
▶ *Adjusted RPR of at least 122, 7/10*
▶ *At least one top-two finish within last two starts, 7/10*
▶ *Rated within 5lb of RPR top-rated, 7/10*
▶ *Drawn in single figures, 7/10*
▶ *Ran in a Classic trial, 6/10*

Other factors
▶ *Six winners had yet to win as a three-year-old*
▶ *Five winners had run in a Guineas*
▶ *Five winners had yet to score over the trip*

that is evident when looking at their two-year-old records. Eighteen of the last 20 winners raced at two but perhaps more telling is the fact that, among them, 14

had a first-four finish at Group level during their juvenile season.

Key races Until recently the trend was for those who had run in a Guineas to hold sway, but Age Of Kings was the first in five years to come down that route. Space Traveller (2019) and Creative Force (2021) had both run in the Listed Carnarvon Stakes at Newbury, finishing third and first, and Noble Truth (2022) had won the Listed King Charles II Stakes at Newmarket.

Trainers Sir Michael Stoute holds the record with six wins and O'Brien is now on four. Godolphin trainers have won three of the last eight runnings.

Betting Six of the last nine winners were in the top three.

Story of the last ten years

	FORM	WINNER	AGE & WGT	Adj RPR	SP	TRAINER	BEST RPR LAST 12 MONTHS (RUNS SINCE)
23	743-0	**Age Of Kings**	3 9-3	113-12	22-1	Aidan O'Brien (IRE)	3rd Tyros Stakes Gp3 (7f) (1)
22	24-01	**Noble Truth** D	3 9-3	125-1	4-1f	Charlie Appleby	won Newmarket Listed (7f) (0)
21	0-111	**Creative Force**	3 9-1	128T	5-1j	Charlie Appleby	won Newbury Listed (6f) (0)
20	2114-	**Molatham** D, BF	3 9-1	123-2	11-2	Roger Varian	won Doncaster Listed (7f) (1)
19	7-237	**Space Traveller**	3 9-1	116-10	25-1	Richard Fahey	2nd Prix Eclipse Gp3 (6f) (5)
18	19-20	**Expert Eye** D	3 9-1	129T	8-1	Sir Michael Stoute	won Vintage Stakes Gp2 (7f) (3)
17	1-12	**Le Brivido**	3 9-1	131T	2-1f	Andre Fabre (FR)	2nd Poule d'Essai des Poulains Gp1 (1m) (0)
16	1-2d3	**Ribchester**	3 9-6	122-5	7-1	Richard Fahey	won Mill Reef Stakes Gp2 (6f) (2)
15	113-7	**Dutch Connection** D	3 9-4	118-9	14-1	Charlie Hills	3rd National Stakes Gp1 (7f) (1)
14	12-13	**Mustajeeb** D	3 9-4	124-4	9-2j	Dermot Weld (IRE)	won Amethyst Stakes Gp3 (1m) (1)

FAVOURITES £3.75

TRAINERS IN THIS RACE (w-pl-r) Charlie Appleby 2-2-7, Richard Fahey 2-0-5, Aidan O'Brien 1-4-16, Roger Varian 1-1-10, Charlie Hills 1-0-7, Sir Michael Stoute 1-2-4, Andre Fabre 1-0-1, Andrew Balding 0-1-6, William Haggas 0-2-7, Saeed bin Suroor 0-0-7, John & Thady Gosden 0-1-5, Richard Hannon 0-0-10

FATE OF FAVOURITES 1061026119 **POSITION OF WINNER IN MARKET** 1621304118

DONATE TODAY

To donate £5, text ROR2 to 70970
To donate £10, text ROR2 to 70191

Help retired racehorses find new purpose and loving homes

We offer retraining and rehoming support, and welfare programmes to make sure racehorses have a dignified and fulfilling life after they stop racing

01488 648998   **DONATE**®   ror.org.uk

ATING back to 1813, this is the last heritage handicap of the week, with up to 30 runners charging down the straight in a hotly contested 6f race.

Last year's winner Saint Lawrence was in the right age and ratings bands but missed other key trends apart from his winning form over 7f, which can help over this testing 6f. The 22-1 shot, having his first run for Archie Watson after a recent switch, had good course form, including sixth place in the previous year's King's Stand Stakes.

Form Ten of the last 18 winners were no more than 2lb off top on Racing Post Ratings. Only four of those 18 had won that season, although 11 had achieved a top-four finish last time out.

Draw Recent runnings suggest the winner can come from anywhere on the track, although by a strange quirk three of the last five winners have come out of stall ten. Saint Lawrence was drawn highest in stall 30 last year.

Weight Winners have tended to come from a narrow weights range, from 8st 12lb to 9st 3lb, although four of the last six have carried more than that.

Key races Ten of the last 18 winners had won or been placed in a field of 18 runners or more. The Victoria Cup at Ascot can be significant, along with the Class 2 6f handicap at York's Dante meeting.

Trainers Newmarket stables have the best long-term record but northern trainers have done well recently, winning three of the last ten runnings.

Betting Even though only two favourites have won since 2005, nine of the 18 winners since then have come from the first four in the market.

Key trends

▸ *Distance winner, 8/10*
▸ *Officially rated between 99 and 107, 8/10*
▸ *Aged four or five, 8/10 (six aged five)*
▸ *Rated within 6lb of RPR top-rated, 7/10 (last three winners the exceptions)*
▸ *Won over 7f, 7/10*
▸ *Top-four finish last time out, 6/10*

Other factors

▸ *Three winners were drawn between 12 and 22, four in one to 11 and three between 23 and 31*
▸ *Five winners had won or placed in a field of at least 16 runners*

Story of the last ten years

	FORM	WINNER	AGE & WGT	OR	SP	TRAINER	BEST RPR LAST 12 MONTHS (RUNS SINCE)
23	00-60	**Saint Lawrence**	5 9-2	100-9	22-1	Archie Watson	6th Abernant Stakes Gp 3 (6f) (1)
22	0-878	**Rohaan** CD	4 9-12	109-9	18-1	David Evans	won Wokingham Handicap (6f) (7)
21	21511	**Rohaan** CD	3 9-8	112-10	8-1	David Evans	won Sandy Lane Stakes Gp2 (6f) (0)
20	000-0	**Hey Jonesy** D	5 9-3	99-1	18-1	Kevin Ryan	2nd Haydock Class 3 conditions (7f) (4)
19	227-1	**Cape Byron** C	5 9-9	107-4	7-2f	Roger Varian	won Victoria Cup hcap (7f) (0)
18	5314-	**Bacchus** D	4 9-6	105-6	33-1	Brian Meehan	won Newmarket Class 2 hcap (6f) (1)
17	7-304	**Out Do** D	8 8-13	99-2	25-1	David O'Meara	3rd Ascot Class 2 hcap (5f) (7)
16	40-70	**Outback Traveller** C, D	5 9-1	100T	10-1	Robert Cowell	4th Ascot Class 2 hcap (7f) (3)
15	413-2	**Interception** D	5 9-3	102-6	10-1	David Lanigan	2nd Haydock Listed (6f) (0)
14	50-22	**Baccarat** D, BF	5 9-2	105T	9-1	Richard Fahey	2nd York Class 2 hcap (6f) (0)

WINS-RUNS 3yo 1-0-1, 4yo 2-12-89, 5yo 6-4-66, 6yo+ 1-14-102 **FAVOURITES** -£5.50

FATE OF FAVOURITES 0528210396 **POSITION OF WINNER IN MARKET** 4440019400

THIS 1m2f handicap for three-year-olds rated 0-105 was introduced as part of the expanded programme in 2020 and has been won by two 20-1 shots (Highland Chief for Paul and Oliver Cole in 2020 and Burdett Road for Michael Bell last year), either side of the Andrew Balding-trained Foxes Tales (2021) at 13-2 and 5-2 favourite Missed The Cut (2022) for George Boughey.

The first three came from double-figure draws in 13- or 14-runner fields, but Burdett Road came out of stall nine last year (chased home by those drawn 17 and 16).

Highland Chief won off top weight from an official rating of 101 but Foxes Tales and Missed The Cut had marks of 93 and 95, and Burdett Road ran off 90. That sort of figure in the low to mid 90s looks ideal.

Burdett Road scores at 20-1 last year

THIS is the longest race of the week at two and three-quarter miles – indeed, the longest run under Flat racing rules – and one of the best loved. With such an emphasis on stamina and with fewer out-and-out stayers in Flat yards nowadays, this race has become quite a battleground between the Flat trainers and the top jumps yards.

Last year's winner Dawn Rising, whose trainer Joseph O'Brien is a top-level operator on the Flat and over jumps, was the successful 2-1 favourite having been third in a Grade 1 novice hurdle over the winter and finished third in a Leopardstown Group 3 on his return to the Flat.

Form Most winners had reached a high level over

Key trends
▶ *Officially rated 90-plus, 10/10*
▶ *Aged six to nine, 10/10*
▶ *Contested a Group or Listed race since last season, 9/10*
▶ *Top-six finish in race over 2m2f-plus, 8/10*
▶ *Rated within 11lb of RPR top-rated, 8/10*
▶ *Adjusted RPR at least 113, 7/10*

Other factors
▶ *Only one winner had tasted victory on the Flat that season*

staying distances. Four of the eight different horses to score in the past decade had finished in the first four in the Cesarewitch and/or the Northumberland Plate (two had won one of them) and another was a Group 2 Doncaster Cup winner. The

others were better known as hurdlers and had won or placed at Grade 1/2 level.

Key races The Chester Cup, Northumberland Plate and Cesarewitch (plus its trial) are important handicap markers, along with Group races such as the Doncaster Cup, Goodwood Cup and Sagaro Stakes.

Trainers Irish champion jumps trainer Willie Mullins has the best record with four wins in the past 12 runnings. Aidan O'Brien runners have to be noted. He won in 2008 with Honolulu and two of his three runners since then have been placed.

Betting Most winners were prominent in the market, with 13 of the last 16 coming from the first four in the betting and nothing bigger than Commissioned (12-1 in 2016) since 2004.

Story of the last ten years

	FORM	WINNER	AGE & WGT	Adj RPR	SP	TRAINER	BEST RPR LAST 12 MONTHS (RUNS SINCE)
23	412/3	**Dawn Rising**	6 9-4	111-8	2-1f	Joseph O'Brien (IRE)	3rd Saval Beg Stakes Gp3 (1m6f) (0)
22	140-0	**Stratum** CD	9 9-7	110-14	10-1	Willie Mullins (IRE)	won Queen Alexandra Stakes (2m5½f) (3)
21	20-15	**Stratum**	8 9-2	127T	4-1	Willie Mullins (IRE)	2nd Lonsdale Cup Gp2 (2m½f) (3)
20	1447-	**Who Dares Wins**	8 9-2	120-1	Evsf	Alan King	4th Prix du Cadran Gp1 (2m4f) (1)
19	13-36	**Cleonte** C	6 9-2	120-6	7-2	Andrew Balding	3rd Sagaro Stakes Gp3 (2m) (1)
18	5668-	**Pallasator** C	9 9-2	124-1	11-2	Gordon Elliott (IRE)	6th Prix Kergorlay Gp2 (1m7f) (1)
17	95-25	**Oriental Fox** CD	9 9-5	117-10	10-1	Mark Johnston	2nd Newmarket Class 2 hcap (1m6f) (1)
16	211/	**Commissioned**	6 9-2	113-11	12-1	Gordon Elliott (IRE)	Seasonal debut (0)
15	3756-	**Oriental Fox**	7 9-2	120-1	4-1	Mark Johnston	6th Northumberland Plate hcap (2m) (0)
14	321-5	**Pique Sous**	7 9-2	108-18	11-4	Willie Mullins (IRE)	won Leopardstown hcap (1m6f) (1)

WINS-RUNS: 4yo 0-6-36, 5yo 0-2-16, 6yo+ 10-12-77 **FAVOURITES**: -£5.00

TRAINERS IN THIS RACE (w-pl-r) Willie Mullins 3-4-12, Gordon Elliott 2-1-3, Andrew Balding 1-1-8, Alan King 1-0-6, Joseph O'Brien 1-0-3, Charlie Appleby 0-0-2, Aidan O'Brien 0-2-3, Ian Williams 0-5-5, Hughie Morrison 0-0-5

FATE OF FAVOURITES 4432631971 **POSITION OF WINNER IN MARKET** 2364321251

From the breeding shed to the racecourse

GREAT BRITISH BONUS

GBB supports British-bred fillies and their connections by awarding bonuses of up to £20,000 per race.

For more information, scan the QR code

#BREEDBUYRACE

Notable double in sight

William Buick on Notable Speech: "I've never sat on a miler with that sort of speed"

NOTABLE SPEECH has already lit up the Flat season and is now in line to become the ninth horse since the turn of the millennium to complete the 2,000 Guineas-St James's Palace double.

The Godolphin colt did not make his debut until the end of January on the all-weather at Kempton but turns towards the royal meeting with a perfect 4-4 record for Charlie Appleby.

Notable Speech was deemed too weak to race at two, despite showing promising signs at home, but he has risen sharply up the ranks this year. A maiden success was followed by two more Kempton victories in conditions events, justifying short-priced favouritism on all three occasions.

Despite his unbeaten record and illustrious connections, Notable Speech went somewhat under the radar into the Guineas with most of the focus on the much-hyped City Of Troy.

On his first start on turf, William Buick's mount made smooth headway on the far side and quickened up smartly to put the race to bed in the style of an above-average Guineas winner.

He matched the Racing Post Rating of 123 achieved by the Godolphin-Appleby 2022 Guineas winner Coroebus, who took the St James's Palace on his next start, while only Gleneagles in 2015 ran to a higher winning figure (124) in the last ten Guineas – and he also went on to land the St James's Palace.

Given all the top-class horses Buick has ridden, it was striking just how blown away he was by his first 2,000 Guineas winner.

"I've never sat on a miler with that sort of pace and speed," he said. "He went past them so easily that I could have sat there longer but when I asked him he just turned on."

What are the potential negatives? Ease underfoot would pose a question mark given his Guineas win came on drying ground described as good, while his dam Swift Rose never raced on a slow surface. The progeny of Notable Speech's sire Dubawi have a better strike-rate on good or good to firm ground.

It can be argued that his Guineas rivals, chiefly runner-up Rosallion, could find more improvement on their second starts of the campaign, but Notable Speech is even less exposed and looks well set to mark himself out as the top miler by backing up his Classic breakthrough.

STAR RATING

★ ★ ★ ★ ★

Hannon eyes turnaround

Rosallion (left) has a length and a half to make up on Notable Speech from their 2,000 Guineas meeting

THE St James's Palace Stakes on the round course at Ascot offers a different test to the 2,000 Guineas on Newmarket's straight Rowley Mile and that gives Richard Hannon plenty of hope for his Classic runner-up Rosallion.

Hannon has previous on this score having won the race with Guineas runner-up Barney Roy, who managed to reverse the Rowley Mile form with Churchill in 2017.

Rosallion has a length and a half to find with Notable Speech from the Guineas but there was plenty to like about his performance.

Sean Levey's mount arguably travelled best to the final furlong and a half on his first start of the campaign, whereas Notable Speech had a race-fitness edge having already run three times at Kempton since the end of January.

Sheikh Obaid's son of Blue Point kept trying all the way to the line and is likely to find further improvement on his second outing of the season and just his second start round a bend. Hannon certainly shares that view.

"In any other year Rosallion did enough to win the Guineas but it was a very deep renewal, probably the best we've seen in ten years," the trainer said. "I don't think there's any way I could say my horse needed the run because he was as fit as a fiddle, and I was very pleased with the way he travelled, the way he ran on and the way he tried.

"The winner is a monster, but I really do think it could be a different story around a bend. There's nothing to lose and everything to gain from taking on Notable Speech again. Our horse has a blinding turn of foot and that could be well used kicking off a bend."

Rosallion had a 3-4 record at two, including victory on his sole visit to Ascot in a red-hot Listed Pat Eddery Stakes in July. Subsequent top-level winners Ancient Wisdom and Sunway were in behind.

His best juvenile performance came on his only start around a bend when a ready length winner of the Group 1 Prix Jean-Luc Lagardere on Arc day at Longchamp. The runner-up Unquestionable franked the form when successful in the Breeders' Cup Juvenile Turf at Santa Anita.

Rosallion raced too keenly on his sole below-par run when third in the Champagne at Doncaster on soft ground last year but he has otherwise been reliable and progressive. There is plenty to like about his chances.

STAR RATING
★★★★

First-class booking

Passenger: ready for a return to the top level after reappearing with a Group 2 win at Chester

SIR MICHAEL STOUTE is the master trainer at taking a patient approach and it looks to be paying off with the talented Passenger. Perhaps this might be another in the mould of Poet's Word and Crystal Ocean, two slow-burners who eventually became Prince of Wales's Stakes winners.

The Niarchos family's homebred son of Ulysses is best remembered at three for a luckless third in last year's Dante at York.

Following a convincing debut success in the Wood Ditton at Newmarket, Passenger was sent off 9-2 favourite for York's Derby trial. Having raced slightly keenly, he was continually denied a run at a crucial stage between the two-furlong and one-furlong poles.

His winning chance was over but Passenger still ran on to force a dead-heat for third with subsequent St Leger scorer Continuous, convincing connections to have a tilt at the Derby.

Passenger was never involved at Epsom, finishing a distant 12th on his only try at 1m4f, and the drop back to 1m2f after a break yielded victory in the Group 3 Winter Hill Stakes at Windsor in August on his final start at three.

It was Passenger's return success in the Group 2 Huxley Stakes at Chester's May meeting that marked him out as ready for a move back to top-level company.

All bar one of Passenger's rivals had a run under their belt but Stoute's colt produced an impressive turn of foot to beat Israr, who was rated 3lb superior, by a length and a half.

His regular rider Richard Kingscote feels there is more to come. "Last year was a little bit stop-start, but he showed nice form on quite a few occasions, and hopefully we'll get a good run with him," he said.

"He was still learning while we were going round there, but I was very happy with him. I thought he did a lot really nicely. It's the sort of race that will bring him forward."

Further improvement is definitely required for Passenger to strike at the top level, but his Huxley win was just his fifth start and, on that evidence, he is only going to get better at four.

Staying at the Prince of Wales's trip – rather than going for the Group 2 Hardwicke over 1m4f – looks the right move and Passenger is very much in the mix despite lacking any genuine Group 1 form.

Passenger is unraced on ground slower than good – so any significant rain would raise a question mark – and hasn't run on a conventional right-handed round course.

With Stoute's approach in mind, though, there will no doubt be more in the locker from this promising work in progress.

STAR RATING
★★★★

91

Elmalka

Big-hearted star filly

> **❝Elmalka is not very big, but she has a big heart. She lengthens very well and when I hit the rising ground she really hit her stride❞**

BACKERS of Elmalka in the Coronation Stakes will be relying on the recent record of 1,000 Guineas winners in the race taking a turn for the better.

Five Newmarket scorers have attempted to win this Group 1 in the past decade and only Winter, who landed the Irish 1,000 Guineas in between Newmarket and Ascot, was successful.

The Aidan O'Brien-trained filly also struck in the Nassau in 2017 and was an above-average 1,000 Guineas winner – a view backed up by Racing Post Ratings as she recorded a Guineas RPR of 117 compared to the ten-year winning average of 116.

Elmalka was awarded an RPR of 113 following her neck success over Porta Fortuna at 28-1 – a rating bettered by recent Guineas winners Billesdon Brook and Cachet, who failed to land the Coronation. She matched the RPR recorded by other Guineas scorers Mother Earth and Hermosa, who were also beaten in this race.

The overall record of Guineas winners in the Coronation since the turn of the millennium is 5-13, with Russian Rhythm, Attraction, Ghanaati and Sky Lantern the others to do the double.

There should definitely be more to come from Elmalka, who made a successful debut on the all-weather at Southwell in November and had her second and third starts in the space of just over a fortnight when third in the Fred Darling at Newbury before winning at Newmarket.

Guineas-winning rider Silvestre de Sousa said: "Elmalka is not very big, but she has a big heart. She lengthens very well and when I hit the rising ground she really hit her stride. They went off quick enough but when she got organised she really got into it."

There is a concern that a mile on the round course on quick ground could be sharp enough for Elmalka.

A strong gallop played to her strengths on the Rowley Mile and there is every chance she will be at her best over further. Her dam Nahrain was a dual top-level winner over 1m2f and, while her sire Kingman was an out-and-out miler, her granddam Bahr was second in the Oaks and won the Ribblesdale over 1m4f, so there is plenty of stamina in the pedigree.

In what appears a potentially open Coronation, there are reasons to take on Elmalka even though she will arrive off a big career-best performance.

STAR RATING
★★★★

Elmalka: will bid to improve the recent poor record of 1,000 Guineas winners in the Coronation Stakes

Auguste Rodin

Owners: M Tabor & D Smith & Mrs J Magnier & Westerberg; Trainer: Aidan O'Brien

Top of the wishlist

IF THERE was one horse on the wishlist for Ascot's flagship meeting, it would surely be Auguste Rodin. He scores top marks as much for suspenseful unpredictability as sheer class.

At his brilliant best last year he won the Derby, Irish Derby, Irish Champion Stakes and Breeders' Cup Turf. Interweaved in that superb record, however, were his 12th of 14 in the 2,000 Guineas and last of ten in the King George at Ascot. This year started with a last of 12 in the Dubai Sheema Classic at Meydan.

A Derby winner running at Royal Ascot the following year is a rare event. Usually it doesn't go too well. The last two Derby winners to turn up at the royal meeting the following season were Masar in 2019 and Anthony Van Dyck in 2020; both finished fifth in the Hardwicke Stakes.

Camelot was fourth in the 2013 Prince of Wales's Stakes, and before him Sir Percy was last of six in the 2007 running of that race.

For the last horse to win at Royal Ascot after landing the Derby, you have to go all the way back to Royal Palace in the 1968 Prince of Wales's.

One issue is that there is no 1m4f Group 1 at the royal meeting and not all Derby winners can be at their best taking on the top 1m2f performers in the Prince of Wales's.

That wouldn't be a problem for Auguste Rodin judged on his brilliant Irish Champion victory over stablemate Luxembourg last September. His Racing Post Rating of 126 was the joint-best of his career alongside his Breeders' Cup win over 1m4f.

Nor would quick ground be an issue. The Breeders' Cup was run on firm and the Derby on good to firm. It's just a question of whether a visit to Royal Ascot fits into Aidan O'Brien's plans.

It would be exciting if it happened. Auguste Rodin at his brilliant best would take the meeting into a different realm.

Auguste Rodin: record shows a mix of brilliant best and woeful worst

STAR RATING
★ ★ ★ ★ ★

Classy and consistent

PORTA FORTUNA has improved for the step up to a mile and a career-best effort could be in the offing at a meeting where she was successful last season.

The Donnacha O'Brien-trained filly was tremendously consistent in a busy seven-race campaign at two. She finished first or second in six of those starts and third in the other.

Porta Fortuna took her record to 3-3 when landing the Albany over 6f at the royal meeting and four subsequent Group winners were in behind.

She was successful at the third attempt in Group 1 company when winning the Cheveley Park over the same trip at Newmarket in September and she matched her Racing Post Rating that day when second on her first try at a mile in the Breeders'

Cup Juvenile Fillies Turf at Santa Anita in November.

A tight track and firm ground assisted Porta Fortuna on that occasion over the trip and, while she was ultimately outstayed by Elmalka on her reappearance

Porta Fortuna: superb record on fast ground could be a factor in the Coronation Stakes

at three in the 1,000 Guineas at Newmarket, she ran a highly creditable race.

An emphasis on stamina in the Classic was not ideal for Porta Fortuna but she was beaten only a neck – an effort that very much suggested she has more to offer, particularly when considering she was the only filly in the first four not to have had a prep run.

O'Brien said: "I was delighted with how she ran at Newmarket. She ran an absolute belter and we had no excuses. Everything went according to plan. She probably didn't get the credit she deserved for all she did last year and it was nice to see she has trained on and ran so well on her first start at three."

Her connections can take encouragement from the record of beaten Guineas horses in the Coronation, with Rizeena (seventh), Alcohol Free (fifth) and last year's runner-up Tahiyra having won in the past decade.

Porta Fortuna, who is also entered in the Commonwealth Cup over 6f, possibly paid for chasing speed horse Ramatuelle at Newmarket, but going round a bend should suit her better and ensure speed becomes a key factor in the home straight.

She won on heavy ground on her debut last year but ease underfoot would be a concern at a mile. Fast ground would be perfect, given her form figures of 112 on good to firm or quicker.

STAR RATING
★★★★

Head-scratcher

INSPIRAL'S head-scratching comeback in the Lockinge Stakes offered more questions than answers in relation to her chances of enhancing her fine record at the royal meeting.

Winner of the Coronation in 2022 and runner-up in last year's Queen Anne, Inspiral has shown some of her best form when fresh, which made her 13-length fourth in the Newbury Group 1 all the more baffling.

It might be the case that the five-year-old takes more work in her later years to reach peak fitness and that she will come on plenty for her reappearance, but there is also a chance she wants further than the mile trip of the Queen Anne.

The Cheveley Park Stud homebred was successful on her first try at 1m2f when winning the Breeders' Cup Filly & Mare Turf at Santa Anita in November and connections were keen to stress the Prince of Wales's Stakes is a viable option for the six-time top-level winner.

Joint-trainer John Gosden said: "The Queen Anne is probably her aim but we will also look at the Prince of Wales's over a mile and a quarter. It's an easy ten furlongs at Santa Anita but she galloped out well there and Frankie [Dettori] couldn't pull her up.

"She came to make her run and just got tired [in the Lockinge]. In her work at home she's a lot older and wiser, and I'm not going to tell her what to do. She needed this race to bring her on for Ascot. I'm delighted with her run."

The Lockinge was won by Audience, who represented the same connections, and his likely participation in the Royal Ascot opener is another reason for the team to consider a step up in trip for Inspiral.

Audience failed to win in four attempts in Group 2 company last season, which made his Lockinge success such a surprise on his first start in a Group 1.

It was also the five-year-old's first run

Owner: Cheveley Park Stud
Trainers: John & Thady Gosden

over a mile and his customary front-running tactics paid off, bringing him home a length and three-quarters ahead of the in-form Charyn.

Audience is unlikely to be given a soft lead in the Queen Anne on the back of his top-level breakthrough, but of more concern is his tendency to show his best form when fresh.

He has form figures of 1211 on his first start of the season but is winless in six runs when the gap from his previous outing was a month or shorter.

STAR RATING
★★★★★

Inspiral: Ascot trip options for six-time Group 1 winner

BOUGHT for a joint-sale-topping 625,000gns at the Craven Breeze-Up last April, Vandeek was the archetypal fast and early two-year-old that type of auction is meant to produce. And much more besides.

In less than six months, he went from breezing at the sales to blitzing all-comers on the track. A perfect 4-4 record over 6f included Group 1 wins in the Prix Morny at Deauville and the Middle Park Stakes at Newmarket and made him the highest-rated British-trained juvenile in the official end-of-year standings.

It was clear to owner Sheikh Khalid bin Hamad Al Khalifa and trainers Simon and Ed Crisford exactly what they had. Vandeek was a grey ball of speed, a sprinter pure and simple.

After the Middle Park, there was no thought of trying to stretch him out in distance in the Dewhurst Stakes. "Sheikh Khalid has decided he would like to keep Vandeek for sprinting next year," said Simon Crisford. "We would like Vandeek to stay at what he's very good at."

Nor was there any intention of running him in a mile Classic. The Commonwealth Cup, put in place in 2015 precisely to offer three-year-old sprinters a Group 1 target in their own age group at Royal

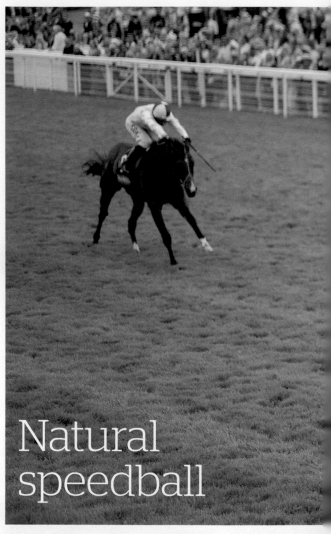

Natural speedball

Ascot, would be the first big aim.

Vandeek holds strong credentials for the 6f contest. The best juvenile Racing Post Rating among the previous nine Commonwealth Cup winners is the 117 achieved by Caravaggio and Advertise – and that is exactly what

Vandeek registered in both of his Group 1 wins.

That puts the son of Havana Grey well ahead of the average juvenile RPR of 111 for Commonwealth Cup winners and he is already close to the race-winning average of 119.

Interestingly, the Morny

Vandeek: dual Group 1
winner last year over 6f

was on very soft ground and the Middle Park on good to firm, but it was always felt Vandeek would thrive on a quicker surface and that certainly seemed to be the case at Newmarket.

James Doyle, who took over on Vandeek for the Middle Park after Andrea Atzeni moved to Hong Kong, became an instant fan.

"He's electric," he said. "He didn't jump from the gate that quick but he travelled super strong and the moment the gap opened, he put it to bed quickly. Not many horses in a Middle Park go down to the Dip travelling as well as he did. He gave me a serious buzz."

That is high praise from a rider who has had three Group 1 sprint wins at Royal Ascot, two of them on the top-class Blue Point.

STAR RATING
★★★★

Specialist performer

Kinross: set for a third crack at the Queen Elizabeth II Jubilee after finishing eighth and seventh in the past two runnings

KINROSS is an Ascot performer, there's no doubt about that. Where there is a question mark is over his ability to shine in high summer at the royal meeting.

The high-class seven-year-old has recorded an impressive 122 on Racing Post Ratings on three occasions, including in the British Champions Sprint at Ascot in October 2022. At the other end of the scale is the 101 he put up when seventh in the Queen Elizabeth II Jubilee Stakes last June, by far his worst display in a Group 1.

Given that Kinross was eighth in the 2022 Jubilee (RPR 113) on his only other visit to Royal Ascot, the question mark will remain until he provides a more positive answer. He will have another chance in his third crack at the race this year.

The 6f contest has been set as the starting point again by trainer Ralph Beckett. Last year he was 6-1 third favourite there on his reappearance but was beaten by five lengths in a race that may have been there for the taking given that victory went to the year-older Khaadem at 80-1.

It was Kinross's only poor performance in another impressive campaign. From there he was third in the July Cup, won back-to-back Group 2s at Goodwood and York, and finished a close Group 1 runner-up in the Prix de la Foret and British Champions Sprint.

His 2023 record was further evidence that he builds momentum as the season goes on, often reaching his peak over 7f and on autumn ground.

His best nine runs on RPRs have come from August 1 onwards. Seven were at his specialist distance of 7f or a mile and the other two over 6f with soft in the going description.

A rainy end to Royal Ascot would be in Kinross's favour. As Beckett said last autumn: "He's much better on softer ground and seven furlongs is his ultimate distance but the stiff six at Ascot on soft ground suits him."

In those conditions he could run a big race. As for his appetite heading into a sixth season of racing, Beckett reported that the signs this spring have been positive.

"He still enjoys every day and is in great shape," he said. "We won't find out whether he's lost any of his boot until we run him, but he'll start in the Jubilee. We know what he likes and it will fall into place for that reason."

If things fall into place at Royal Ascot, he would be a hugely popular winner.

STAR RATING
★★★★

Big hope for Appleby

BIG EVS will bid to emulate Lady Aurelia and Bradsell by winning the King Charles III Stakes (formerly known as the King's Stand) at three, but does his form meet the required standard?

The 2017 and 2023 winners were among 22 three-year-olds to contest this sprint in the last decade and, like Big Evs, arrived with winning form from the previous year's meeting.

Lady Aurelia landed the Queen Mary at two by seven lengths and Bradsell won the Coventry Stakes. They recorded Racing Post Ratings of 123 and 111, whereas Big Evs registered a figure of 106 when successful in the Windsor Castle.

Mick Appleby's stable star had a busier juvenile campaign than those two sprinters, culminating in a Grade 1 success in the Breeders' Cup Juvenile Turf Sprint at Santa Anita. He recorded an RPR of 113 there but, despite having two Royal Ascot winners in behind, the form has not worked out.

Big Evs returned with a comfortable victory under Tom Marquand in Listed company at York's Dante meeting, giving 5lb and a beating to notably inferior rivals.

The length-and-a-half success at the very least proved Big Evs' wellbeing and connections were pleased with his performance.

Appleby said: "He's not grown much but he's filled out a lot. He's like a bull now and Tom said he's as good as he was in California, if not better.

"From two to three you just never know, but he was showing the signs at home that he's still got it and he showed us that on the track."

That took Big Evs up to an RPR of 116 but a big career-best performance will probably be required in a race where the last seven winners have recorded RPRs of 121-plus, headed by 2022 winner Nature Strip with a standout 129.

Big Evs' last two victories have proved he does not have to blitz his rivals from the front, having taken a lead on both occasions, and that versatility could be an asset in this likely big-field sprint.

Underfoot conditions are no concern for Big Evs backers. The son of Blue Point is 2-2 on soft ground and a winner on good, good to firm and firm.

The main question is whether he can bridge the class gap in his acid test at the top level at three.

STAR RATING
★★★★

Big Evs winning on his return at York and (right) with Mick Appleby

Back in the fray

KYPRIOS will have to emulate Kayf Tara, the only stayer in the modern era to regain the Gold Cup crown, if he is to strike for a second time in Thursday's feature.

Kayf Tara, a neck winner over Double Trigger in 1998, was third behind Enzeli the following year but struck again in 2000 when defeating Far Cry by a head.

The five horses who have attempted to regain the Gold Cup since have been unsuccessful. Mr Dinos and Trip To Paris were well beaten at big odds in 2005 and 2017, while Order Of St George, also trained by Aidan O'Brien, was fourth to Stradivarius in 2018 as the 7-4 joint-favourite.

Stradivarius, a three-time Gold Cup winner, was beaten in the race for the first time in 2021 and could

finish only third as the 2-1 second favourite in 2022, while the 2021 winner Subjectivist, who had a similar profile to Kyprios in coming back from injury to contest the race again, finished a creditable third as the 9-2 second favourite last year.

Subjectivist had a 618-day layoff before runs in Saudi Arabia and Meydan teed up his Gold Cup bid last year, whereas there is more evidence to go on with Kyprios.

An infection on the inside of a joint led O'Brien to believe Kyprios would miss the whole of last season but the star stayer returned towards the back end, finishing second to Eldar Eldarov in the Irish St Leger at the Curragh and filling the same position behind Trawlerman in the Long Distance Cup at Ascot.

His effort on British Champions Day matched his Gold Cup-winning Racing Post Rating of 120 in 2022. Although he recorded higher figures that year when going on to win the Goodwood Cup, Irish St Leger and Prix du Cadran (with a top RPR of 128), his Ascot performance boosted confidence about Kyprios retaining most if not all of his ability.

Kyprios has proved his wellbeing with two wins this campaign, justifying short odds in the Vintage Crop at Navan and the Saval Beg at Leopardstown, after which O'Brien said: "Ryan [Moore] said all the speed is still there and he was just lazy when he got to the front, but that's always been his way. We think he's in a good place."

While those who have recently tried to regain the Gold Cup have failed, it is hard to shake the feeling that a big performance is in the offing from Kyprios.

STAR RATING
★ ★ ★ ★

Kyprios: back to winning form this year in Gold Cup warm-ups at Navan and Leopardstown

Reigning title-holder

COURAGE MON AMI seeks to become the fourth horse since the turn of the millennium to win back-to-back Gold Cups.

That feat has been achieved by Royal Rebel, Yeats – the most successful stayer in the race's illustrious history – and Stradivarius in that period.

Gold Cup winners bidding for consecutive victories in the meeting's most famous race have a 43 per cent strike-rate (6-14) since 2000.

In recent years, Stradivarius was thwarted in his bid for a fourth Gold Cup success when fourth in 2021, while that year's winner Subjectivist and the 2022 scorer Kyprios missed the next running due to injury.

Among the most high-profile beaten previous winners, Estimate finished second – before being disqualified for the presence of a prohibited substance in her sample – in 2014 and Order Of St George was narrowly denied by Big Orange when an odds-on favourite in 2017.

So how did Courage Mon Ami's Gold Cup victory compare to the previous decade? The answer is quite encouraging, with Wathnan Racing's stayer hitting the ten-year winning Racing Post Rating average of 120 on just his fourth start.

Frankie Dettori's mount travelled notably well and saw out the 2m4f trip strongly to beat Coltrane by three-quarters of a length.

His Gold Cup success took his record to 4-4 and the expectation was he would become the dominant force in the staying division. It didn't pan out that way on his final two starts of last season.

The Goodwood Cup, in which all-the-way winner Quickthorn slipped the field, was a first defeat for Courage Mon Ami. He never figured in sixth, which most likely was due to how the race panned out, although it did coincide with the first time he encountered cut in the ground.

Courage Mon Ami's second to Coltrane in the Lonsdale Cup at York – giving the winner 3lb – was more encouraging, although it gave further evidence that there is little to split the Gold Cup one-two.

The Gosdens' latest star stayer did his best work late on the Knavesmire in the 2m½f race and it might just be that the more testing Gold Cup trip helps bring out his best.

Joint-trainer John Gosden said: "He ran a nice race but he ran out of track. Look at the form of the Gold Cup and he had a 3lb penalty – and 3lb over two miles. That was the difference. A little more distance would have suited him too."

STAR RATING
★★★★

Owner: Wathnan Racing
Trainers: John & Thady Gosden

Courage Mon Ami wins
last year's Gold Cup
from Coltrane on only
his fourth career start

Bred for the top

AFTER a perfect three-race campaign as a juvenile, Henry Longfellow got his lines wrong for the first time on his reappearance in the French 2,000 Guineas. Aidan O'Brien blamed himself, however, and quickly pointed the blue-blooded colt towards the St James's Palace Stakes.

Henry Longfellow's sire Dubawi and dam Minding both won mile Classics but the task proved beyond their son at Longchamp, where he was a well-backed 13-10 favourite but finished a tame eighth after a difficult trip under Ryan Moore.

O'Brien felt the patient tactics employed at Longchamp backfired. "It was a tactical error on my behalf," he said. "I said to Ryan to take his time on him because it was his first run and he hadn't run on that type of track before. Then Ryan couldn't get out and as he kept coming back to get out, they kept coming by him and then he was too far back in a slowly run race."

Four of O'Brien's nine St James's Palace winners were beaten in a Guineas. They include Black Minnaloushe

(2001) and Excellent Art (2007), who were sixth and fourth in the French 2,000 before winning at Royal Ascot, and the trainer was looking to tread the same path with Henry Longfellow.

"The horse was very happy in himself afterwards," he said. "He went right-handed, which was a lovely experience, and I would say he felt it was only a piece of work. The plan was to go to the St James's Palace, so we'll stick to that. I'll probably have more confidence to say to Ryan to go forward."

Henry Longfellow showed his Group 1 quality as a two-year-old, winning the National Stakes by five lengths on going that was close to soft. Earlier wins had come over the same Curragh 7f with give in the ground, which his dam handled well too.

O'Brien described him after the National as "a special horse" and there is still plenty of time to restore that reputation. A wet start to Royal Ascot week might help in that quest.

STAR RATING
★ ★ ★ ★

Owners: Michael Tabor & Derrick Smith & Mrs John Magnier
Trainer: Aidan O'Brien

Henry Longfellow: heads
to St James's Palace Stakes
after French Guineas loss

Elite Status

Owner: Sheikh Mohammed Obaid Al Maktoum
Trainer: Karl Burke

Back with a bang

ELITE STATUS was an unconsidered 50-1 shot for the Commonwealth Cup before his reappearance but was dramatically cut to a single-figure price after bouncing right back to form with victory in the Listed Carnarvon Stakes at Newbury.

His juvenile campaign ended on a couple of below-par efforts, although he might have found very soft ground too testing in the Prix Morny at Deauville and the Middle Park appeared to be a race too many on his final start at two.

Those Group 1 outings came after a Group 3 win in France, a close third in the Norfolk Stakes at the royal meeting and victories on his first two starts in a Doncaster maiden and the National Stakes at Sandown, which he landed by five lengths.

Despite his form slightly tailing off at two, Elite Status was not unbacked for his return at Newbury and the money proved well placed.

Clifford Lee's mount travelled strongly, kicked on two furlongs out and was never in any serious danger, beating last season's Queen Mary runner-up Relief Rally by two and three-quarter lengths.

Lee said: "He's had the winter to mentally and physically strengthen up. He's been working really well and feels stronger. He's a big horse with a big stride – I was impressed with him."

The Carnarvon Stakes has provided two of the last six Commonwealth Cup winners, with Eqtidaar finishing fourth at Newbury before winning at the royal meeting in 2018 and Shaquille completing the Carnarvon-Commonwealth Cup double last year. Interestingly, on the same going description of good, Elite Status recorded a quicker time than Shaquille.

On last season's evidence it is hard to envisage Elite Status turning the form around with leading Commonwealth Cup fancy Vandeek, but Karl Burke's talented sprinter might prove a different proposition in top-level races this campaign.

STAR RATING
★★★

Elite Status: major market mover after Newbury victory

VINTAGE SILK TOP HAT RETAIL EVENT

At the **Chesterfield Hotel, Charles St. Mayfair W1**
18th & 19th June.

Alternatively you can come and see us at our workshops in Gloucestershire or Kent.

There's still time to get your own hat repaired.

Before...   ...After

Frogmarsh Mill, South Woodchester,
Stroud, Gloucestershire, GL5 5ET
Tel: 01453 873595
www.honrihats.co.uk

Owner: Al Mohamediya Racing
Trainer: Clive Cox

Confidence restored

"BANG up there with the top juveniles I've had potentially," was Clive Cox's assessment after Jasour's victory in the Group 2 July Stakes last summer.

It was quite a statement considering one of those top juveniles was Golden Horde, also a Group 2 winner at two before going on to Group 1 glory at Royal Ascot in the 2020 Commonwealth Cup.

Cox has long felt Jasour is cut from similar cloth, although his faith was tested when his budding star beat just one horse in Group 1 company in his last two starts of 2023.

The trainer felt the colt's over-keenness in those races was down to a lack of confidence and set about restoring it over the winter. The first fruits of his labour were evident when Jasour reappeared with a decisive win in the Commonwealth Cup Trial at Ascot on May 1.

Cox left no doubt that Jasour is still "bang up there" in his eyes. "I hold him in high regard and I love him," he said. "When things didn't go right last year, it's about keeping everything intact. It was a real project through the winter and the spring, so I'm pleased it seems to be working."

Having Jim Crowley back on board for the first time since the July Stakes was a help and Jasour settled comfortably in the Ascot trial. Most impressively, he showed a lightning turn of foot to score by a length and three-quarters from in-form favourite Adaay In Devon, a Listed winner on her previous start.

The Ascot success came on good to soft ground but it is likely Jasour will be seen to even better effect on faster going, having scored his two juvenile wins on good to firm.

A course-and-distance victory boosts his credentials for the Commonwealth Cup and Cox has every reason to be hopeful again.

"We know he's talented," he said. "He's really got his confidence back and I hope we can keep building it. He's certainly a classy colt."

STAR RATING
★★★

Jasour: back on winning form in Commonwealth Cup Trial at Ascot

Moss Tucker

MOSS TUCKER was the best he has ever been on his reappearance at Naas in April. It was a strong sign that his remarkable progress from long-time handicapper to Group 1-winning sprinter is not over yet.

Unraced at two, the Ken Condon-trained gelding took almost two full seasons to reach the top level, finishing fifth in the 2022 Prix de l'Abbaye. In his second tilt 11 months later, he landed the Flying Five at the Curragh last September to confirm his arrival as a Group 1 sprinter.

That took him to a Racing Post Rating of 118, a far cry from the 57 he recorded with a debut fifth in a 1m2f Cork maiden early in his three-year-old campaign. By the end of that first season he was a confirmed sprinter with an RPR of 100, a 43lb rise.

The next season Moss Tucker went up another 13lb on RPRs and last year he rose again by 5lb. This season he stepped up immediately with an RPR of 120 for his first-time-out Naas Listed win. In another sign of his progress, it was the first time he had won on his seasonal debut.

Condon has entered his stable star in both Group 1 sprints at Royal Ascot and bookmakers make him a touch shorter for the King Charles III Stakes over 5f.

Moss Tucker: Group 1 winner in the Flying Five

Major improver

That is probably his best trip, although he is a Group 3 winner over 6f and his maiden success came at 7½f before he was dropped to sprinting.

The ground is likely to be the deciding factor for Condon. Moss Tucker's two standout performances have come with yielding in the description and heavy has featured for three of his nine wins. The trainer said he will be looking for ground with "kindness in it".

Granted the right conditions, Moss Tucker is quick, tough and determined. And possibly still improving.

STAR RATING
★★★

MILL STREAM was in full flow in two of the main build-up sprints on the way to Royal Ascot, raising hope that this could be his year for a top-level breakthrough for Jane Chapple-Hyam.

As a three-year-old he signed off last season with somewhat disappointing Group 1 efforts – sixth in the Haydock Sprint Cup and eighth in the British Champions Sprint at Ascot – but he has shown enough this spring to suggest he can give a much better account in the Queen Elizabeth II Jubilee Stakes on the final day of the royal meeting.

Following a wind operation over the winter, Mill Stream reappeared at Newmarket in April in the

Fast steps forward

Mill Stream

Owner: PW Harris
Trainer: Jane Chapple-Hyam

Group 3 Abernant Stakes, which has been a stepping stone for several Group 1 sprinters in recent years, including Oxted and Emaraaty Ana. He fought hard but was beaten three-quarters of a length by Washington Heights, another progressive four-year-old en route to the QEII Jubilee.

They met again a month later in the Group 2 Duke of York Stakes and this time victory went to Mill Stream, with Washington Heights half a length back in fourth. Champions Sprint winner Art Power was fifth on his return to British action.

The form looks solid and Mill Stream recorded a career-best 118 on Racing Post Ratings. William Buick, his York jockey, was impressed.

"He really put his head out," he said. "He's been knocking on the door quite a few times and I hope this will be his year. As a four-year-old, he's a big, strong, more mature horse."

Mill Stream is an exciting challenger for owner Peter Harris, a leisure industry billionaire who became a Royal Ascot-winning trainer before his retirement 20 years ago. Having sold his entire racing stock in 2011, he is deeply involved again and has had horses with Chapple-Hyam for the last two and a half years.

"Mr Harris has landed me with some nice horses," the trainer said. "I'm in a lucky position. I have 18 for him. I think Mill Stream's good enough to go to Ascot for the Jubilee."

Considering the QEII Jubilee was won last year with an RPR of 118 and Mill Stream is near the top of this year's ratings, he looks a serious contender.

Mill Stream (white cap, centre) wins the Group 2 Duke of York Stakes

STAR RATING
★★★

Rogue Lightning

Owner: Wathnan Racing
Trainer: Tom Clover

Big-money purchase

ROGUE LIGHTNING certainly made his mark at Ascot last year. He won the Shergar Cup Dash in August and two months later was bought for an eyewatering £1 million in the Champions Day Sale by the emerging force of Wathnan Racing.

He should have plenty more to offer in the sprinting division this campaign and the King Charles III Stakes is the likely target for the Tom Clover-trained four-year-old, who proved a revelation for owners The Rogues Gallery in 2023.

Rogue Lightning showed plenty of promise at two, winning on his debut at Newmarket and finishing second in a Listed race at Newbury, but a tendency to overrace started to become his undoing.

Following a down-the-field ninth in a Newmarket handicap in May last year, the decision was taken to geld the son of Kodiac. He has recorded triple-figure Racing Post Ratings ever since.

The application of a hood has also played its part, with Rogue Lightning's ability to switch off enabling him to show an eyecatching turn of foot when it matters most.

An easy handicap success at Doncaster in July was followed by his convincing Shergar Cup win and Clover's stable star then took his form to the next level when landing the four-runner Listed Scarbrough Stakes back on Town Moor in September.

He beat a reliable yardstick in the now-retired Raasel and that effort earned him a first crack at top-level company in the Prix de l'Abbaye at Longchamp on Arc day in October. He proved to be a major eyecatcher.

Rogue Lightning started from the widest stall and was held up in a race where not many made their presence felt from the rear of the field.

Robert Havlin's mount was denied a clear run two furlongs out but weaved his way through to excellent effect, finishing a never-nearer fifth to Highfield Princess but less than half a length behind the runner-up.

Given the improvement he showed during his three-year-old campaign, and with a record of four wins, a second and a third from nine starts, there should be plenty more to come for new connections this term.

Backing Rogue Lightning does come with risks. His supporters, and most importantly Wathnan's number-one rider James Doyle, will be relying on the gaps opening up given his running style, and the King Charles III has tended to favour those who race up with the pace. Only Oxted and Sole Power have won from the rear in the past decade.

STAR RATING
★ ★ ★

Rogue Lightning: rising sprinter was bought for £1m by Wathnan Racing

Owner: Future Champions Racing Regional
Trainer: Ed Bethell

Bargain star

ED BETHELL took over the training licence from his father James at Thorngill Stables in Middleham at the start of 2021. A few months later, his first Group 1 winner was in the North Yorkshire yard for the bargain price of 3,500gns.

Regional, purchased out of Richard Fahey's stable at the Tattersalls July Sale that year, took 14 races and more than two years to take his young trainer to the top table but he got there last September with a thrilling neck victory in the Haydock Sprint Cup.

It was not only a first Group 1 for Bethell but also for jockey Callum Rodriguez and the ownership syndicate, Future Champions Racing.

By that stage Regional had repaid his purchase price more than a hundred times over with racecourse earnings in excess of £400,000. That figure would take another huge leap if he added another Group 1 victory in one of Royal Ascot's big sprints.

It is a more than realistic aim. Regional achieved a Racing Post Rating of 118 for his Haydock victory and that puts him among the top half-dozen across the two races.

The King Charles III Stakes over 5f could be the slightly easier option and the bookmakers have Regional shortest for that race. His Group 1 win came over the Queen Elizabeth II Jubilee trip of 6f but he certainly has the speed for the shorter race, having set a 5f course record at Haydock on good to firm last June.

One of the key factors in the six-year-old's rise to the top was Rodriguez's work in getting him out of the stalls quickly by whipping off the stalls blindfold at the last moment.

The rider explained: "You're looking at the starter and waiting for the flag to come down and it's all about trying to time it perfectly. He was the first one out at Haydock and took a length or two out of everybody from the stalls."

Having become such a polished sprinter, Regional should be a leading light again.

STAR RATING
★★★

Regional sticks out his neck for Group 1 victory at Haydock in September

Owner: Nurlan Bizakov
Trainer: Roger Varian

Building blocks

CHARYN was the only one of the fancied runners to get anywhere near surprise winner Audience in the Lockinge Stakes at Newbury.

In normal circumstances, second place in a Group 1 would look solid form to take to the Queen Anne Stakes at Royal Ascot, but it was a strange race.

Most won't expect the form to hold up and that leaves the Roger Varian-trained four-year-old still with something to prove at the top level. He does seem progressive, however.

A Group 2 winner at two, he was highly tried at a mile as a three-year-old. He was eighth in the 2,000 Guineas and fourth in the Irish version behind Paddington, then twice third behind that top miler in the St James's Palace and Sussex Stakes. Even when he was dropped a level to the Group 2 Celebration Mile at Goodwood, he was still only third.

This season started better with a Listed win at Doncaster. Like his Group 2 victory at two, that came on soft ground. "He's a bigger, stronger horse this year," said Varian. "We were always keen to drop a level and get a win on the board, then build him back up again."

The building continued with Group 2 success in the Sandown Mile on good to soft. That earned a tilt at the Lockinge, where he finished six and a half lengths clear of the rest but a length and three-quarters behind Audience.

That seemingly took him back to the role of solid placegetter he had played throughout 2023 and it might have been a golden opportunity missed at the top level.

Rider Silvestre de Sousa struck a positive note, though. "There will be a big day in Charyn. A stiff mile will suit him," he said.

Ascot has a stiff mile and the Queen Anne is a big day. Another opportunity awaits.

Charyn: Pattern wins have come with cut in the ground

STAR RATING
★★★

From Vase to Cup

A FEW years ago John Gosden won the Queen's Vase with a promising three-year-old stayer and brought him back 12 months later to land the Gold Cup.

Now, in partnership with his son Thady, he is set to try for the same double with Gregory.

The previous success, of course, came with Stradivarius, who went from Queen's Vase winner in 2017 to Gold Cup hat-trick hero in the next three years.

Gregory has a long way to go even to approach the feats of that much-loved stayer but the first steps have been promising.

After landing the Queen's Vase on only his third start, he was third in the Great Voltigeur and fifth in the St Leger – both times behind Continuous – and returned this year with another third place on the Knavesmire in the Yorkshire Cup.

The son of Golden Horn appeared to hit a flat spot as the race began in earnest two furlongs out but then ran on well. He was too late to catch Giavellotto, winning the race for a second year, but gave the impression a stronger staying test would suit him.

The Gold Cup trip is

Gregory: promising winner of last year's Queen's Vase

three-quarters of a mile further than he's gone before and that is nearly always a big unknown with any first-timer in the race.

There is also the question of whether he can beat stablemate Courage Mon Ami, who races in the same colours and has the 'been there, done that' T-shirt from last year's Gold Cup.

Yet Gosden snr saw

distinct promise in the Yorkshire Cup. "I really liked the way Gregory got his second wind and stayed on again. The plan is to go straight to the Gold Cup. He'll enjoy the distance."

STAR RATING
★★★

'He has plenty of speed'

WHISTLEJACKET

Painters and works of art are a strong theme among the latest crop of Ballydoyle two-year-olds and Whistlejacket looked a picture with a stunning Listed success on his second start at the Curragh.

Named after the famous horse portrait by George Stubbs, the 500,000gns yearling purchase quickened clear by three and three-quarter lengths from four rivals, three of whom were maiden winners.

The impressive display also took the Aidan O'Brien-trained colt clear in the two-year-old rankings with a Racing Post Rating of 101, which is already close to a Royal Ascot winning mark. Only ten juveniles broke three figures at last year's meeting.

The son of No Nay Never has a Royal Ascot pedigree too, being a brother to 2022 Windsor Castle winner Little Big Bear, who returned last year to finish second in the Commonwealth Cup.

Given his connections, it was no surprise Whistlejacket was sent off even-money favourite on his debut over 6f at the Curragh in April but, despite travelling strongly on the soft/heavy ground, he was beaten two and a half lengths by the promising Cowardofthecounty.

Dropped to 5f a fortnight later and this time a 5-6 shot, he made all on the soft ground and went clear before the furlong pole to score comfortably.

The Windsor Castle won by his brother is over 5f or he could go back up in trip for the Coventry, and it was no surprise O'Brien was non-committal after the Curragh win.

"Whistlejacket is one we thought would win first time but we're very happy with that," he said. "He could go five or six – he has plenty of speed."

The ground could be the deciding factor. Little Big Bear's two Royal Ascot runs were both on good to firm and his brother may well enjoy faster conditions too.

COWARDOFTHECOUNTY

Joseph O'Brien unleashed a pair of potentially top-class juveniles in consecutive maidens at the Curragh on April 21 and both first-time-out winners could line up at Royal Ascot.

The most impressive on the day was Cowardofthecounty, a physically imposing colt who not only reeled in the well-touted Whistlejacket but powered two and a half lengths clear on the soft/heavy ground over 6f. There was another six and a half lengths back to the third.

O'Brien liked what he saw from the son of Kodi Bear. "He couldn't have been more impressive," he said. "He's big, well over 500kg, which for a two-year-old at this stage is a lot. This fella looked like he could be a bit special at home but you're never really sure with a two-year-old until they go to the races."

The trainer was just as pleased with Cowardofthecounty's progress at home after his debut – making him inclined to head straight to the Coventry – and with how the form was franked by Whistlejacket's Listed win a fortnight later.

"Whistlejacket looked really good and it's exciting to have a horse in his league," he told At The Races.

Anything in that league looks set to be premier level at the royal meeting.

LEADING JUVENILES

Horse	Trainer	RPR
Whistlejacket	Aidan O'Brien	101
The Actor	Richard Hannon	92
Camille Pissarro	Aidan O'Brien	91
Tropical Storm	Andrew Balding	91
Andesite	Karl Burke	90
Cowardofthecounty	Joseph O'Brien	90
Hawaiian	Richard Hannon	90
Make Haste	Diego Dias	90
Scorthy Champ	Joseph O'Brien	90
Symbol Of Honour	Charlie Appleby	90

*Up to and including May 17

MIDNIGHT STRIKE

The other two-year-old maiden winner for Joseph O'Brien at the Curragh on April 21 was Midnight Strike, perhaps more surprisingly than Cowardofthecounty but also impressively by two lengths over 5f.

"I thought he was a nice colt, but I didn't expect him to win like he did," O'Brien admitted. "He looks an Ascot type. We thought he'd stay six furlongs but was certainly quick enough to start at five. He looks smart."

It was a significant positive for O'Brien to win with the first two juvenile colts he had run this season, given that he is not a trainer to test out his youngsters with an older horse to see what he has.

"This is just the second time they've been on grass," he said. "We don't drill our two-year-olds and like them to progress. It bodes well."

HAWAIIAN

Spring maidens at Newbury are often a springboard to Royal Ascot, given the strength of the stables in the area, and the 5f contest won by the Richard Hannon-trained Hawaiian on April 19 looks one to note.

Sheikh Mohammed Obaid's homebred son of Kodiac was all the rage in the market and justified 11-8 favouritism, albeit by only a neck after showing signs of greenness. He stumbled at the start and hung right near the end, but in between there was plenty to like about his strong-travelling style and the way he responded to a challenge to get home on the good to soft ground.

A Racing Post Rating of 90 was a smart showing for a debutant and the form stood up well. Runner-up Star Anthem scored by four lengths next time, the fourth Running Queen also won and the fifth Tropical Storm was a close second to Hawaiian's stablemate The Actor in a good novice at Newmarket.

The market confidence behind Hawaiian was no surprise given Hannon's post-race comments. "He did a bit of work at Kempton and I thought it was a little bit too good to be true," he told At The Races.

"He's very fast and I hope he's an Ascot horse. I think he'll improve a lot from that, like all ours do."

Cowardofthecounty leads Whistlejacket before scoring at the Curragh in April

'Definitely one for Ascot'

CAMILLE PISSARRO

Price tag, pedigree and performance all point to this son of Wootton Bassett being one of Aidan O'Brien's better two-year-olds, especially in terms of Royal Ascot.

The 1.25m gns colt is a half-brother to Golden Horde, who won the 2020 Commonwealth Cup for Clive Cox having been a high-class juvenile with victory in the Group 2 Richmond Stakes and placed efforts at the top level.

It was perhaps significant that Camille Pissarro made his debut in the same 6f maiden at Navan won 12 months earlier by River Tiber, who went on to land the Coventry Stakes at Royal Ascot, and there was strong market confidence.

The 10-11 favourite duly delivered, although the race did not go entirely smoothly. He dwelt a little at the start and ran green for Ryan Moore when asked for his effort from a furlong out, although he was well on top by a length and a half at the line.

Stable representative Chris Armstrong made clear that Camille Pissarro is held in high regard at Ballydoyle. He said: "The penny only really started to drop with him in the last furlong, which was the best part of the race for him. He's definitely one for Ascot. Once he can put a front nine and a back nine together, he's very exciting with a fantastic attitude."

Golden Horde ran fifth in the Coventry early in his two-year-old career but much better will be expected of his well-touted half-brother.

MOUNTAIN BREEZE

The most recent of Godolphin's infrequent runners in the Albany Stakes was 2022 runner-up Mawj and that raises interest in Mountain Breeze, who was quick to be pointed in that direction by trainer Charlie Appleby.

Mawj went on to be a star at three for Saeed bin Suroor, winning the 1,000 Guineas and a US Grade 1, and the Albany could also be a stepping stone to better things for the three-parts-sister to Appleby's brilliant Pinatubo.

Mountain Breeze made an excellent start in a 5f fillies' novice on 1,000 Guineas day at Newmarket and looked even better upped to the Albany trip of 6f back there a fortnight later, scoring decisively both times.

Immediately after the first win, Appleby nominated the Albany for the daughter of Lope De Vega. "We came here with confidence as her work had been good and she's a well-bred filly. Her class got her through as she hated every minute of the track," he said.

Pinatubo won the Chesham for Appleby in a stellar juvenile campaign in 2019 and the trainer certainly knows how to line up a Royal Ascot two-year-old.

ENCHANTING EMPRESS

Kia Joorabchian's Amo Racing broke their Royal Ascot duck last year with 150-1 Norfolk Stakes winner Valiant Force and this time it could be the turn of Dominic Ffrench Davis, one of the trainers in whom Joorabchian has placed his trust.

The Lambourn trainer reached a career-best 23 winners last year in his 30th campaign and will have high hopes of improving again given the Amo ammunition.

Enchanting Empress set the early standard among his youngsters with victory in the Royal Ascot Two-Year-

Camille Pissarro stretches out to score on his debut at Navan

Old Trial on May 1, making it two out of two over 5f under David Egan after all-weather success at Wolverhampton on her debut three weeks earlier.

A step up to 6f is on the cards in the Albany at Royal Ascot. "She will definitely get six and will probably go further in time," the trainer told At The Races after the trial. "It's a fast pedigree, but she was behind the bridle at Wolverhampton and again a little bit here. She's as tough as old boots and she answered when David asked her, so I think the Albany is probably her target."

UNEXPECTED ISSUES

The money spoke in favour of the Fozzy Stack-trained Unexpected Issues on her debut in a strong-looking 5f maiden at Navan and the daughter of Starspangledbanner justified the confidence with a half-length victory.

Stack also trained the filly's brother Castle Star, a fast and early juvenile in 2021 who didn't go to Royal Ascot but was a Group 3 winner and ended his campaign with a close second to Perfect Power in the Group 1 Middle Park Stakes.

The 6f Albany Stakes looks the likely target for Unexpected Issues.

"She was a little bit green, a little bit slow away and then ran around a bit. She should come forward for that. She'd only worked once on grass," Stack said after her debut.

"Castle Star was a very good horse and he got beaten first time out, so she's already done better than him. I would say she'll get six furlongs now."

> **66** It's a fast pedigree, but she was behind the bridle at Wolverhampton and again a little bit here. She's as tough as old boots and I think the Albany is probably her target **99**

125

'Class from the first day'

GABALDON

The link between Royal Ascot and Gulfstream Park had an instant dividend last year when Crimson Advocate went on from one of the 'win and you're in' juvenile qualifiers at the Florida track to land the Queen Mary Stakes.

Bullet, the fillies' qualifier winner this year, isn't travelling, so it will be the turn of Gabaldon to try to cash in one of the golden tickets after his all-the-way success in the Royal Palm Juvenile on May 11.

The Jose D'Angelo-trained debutant was fast out of the gate and opened a clear lead at the top of the stretch to score by a length and a quarter. The son of Gone Astray completed the 5f in 56.20sec, 0.6sec faster than Bullet in the other qualifier, although the filly had a much more troubled passage.

"He showed class from the first day and he's never missed a workout," D'Angelo said. "We were looking for a horse to run in this race. Now we're looking for a [top] hat."

Last year's Royal Palm Juvenile winner, No Nay Mets, went on to finish ninth in the Norfolk Stakes and the choice for D'Angelo appears to lie between that race and the Windsor Castle Stakes, the other 5f juvenile contest open to colts.

MAKE HASTE

Brazilian trainer Diego Dias has been operating from his County Kildare base for barely a year but has already made a splash in Britain and now has a live candidate for the Queen Mary Stakes in Make Haste.

Last summer Dias had a 20-1 maiden winner at Glorious Goodwood with his first British runner and in Ireland he has had Group and Listed places from just a handful of runners, suggesting a Pattern win might not be far away.

He is backed by Star Bloodstock, having prepared their horses for four years before taking out his training licence. Managing partner Matt Eves is a co-owner of Make Haste, who made an impressive debut at Naas in May when she took a 5f maiden by three and a quarter lengths.

The daughter of Blue Point was well backed but looked like she would improve physically and mentally, having being led by two handlers in the parade ring.

She raced keenly in the early stages but sprinted clear in the final furlong under Gavin Ryan.

Dias said: "We thought a lot of Make Haste at home. Gavin said they could only take her to the three-furlong pole and after that he just had to let her go. We like to think she's a Queen Mary filly."

SPARKLING SEA

Ger Lyons' sole Royal Ascot success came with Elletelle in the 2007 Queen Mary Stakes and now he has high hopes again with another fast filly in Sparkling Sea.

Much has changed for Lyons since 2007. Back then he was sending out around 25-30 winners a season but

Make Haste: big Queen Mary hope for Diego Dias

now he is a Classic-winning trainer who regularly has triple that number and is backed by some of the biggest owners.

Sparkling Sea is a Moyglare Stud homebred who lived up to the first part of her name on her debut in a 6f Naas fillies' maiden on yielding ground in late April. The daughter of Starspangledbanner sped away from Ballydoyle's odds-on Fairy Godmother to score by two and a half lengths under Colin Keane.

Fairy Godmother reversed the placings, albeit by only a neck, when they met again over the same course and distance in the Group 3 Fillies Sprint Stakes three weeks later.

A third clash looks on the cards in the Albany Stakes at Royal Ascot and clearly the pair are two of the best early juvenile fillies in Ireland.

Lyons says the fillies are smart among what he describes as a lovely bunch of two-year-olds in his yard, and this one could be the smartest of the lot at this stage.

STAR ANTHEM

Clive Cox has sent out three juvenile winners at Royal Ascot – a couple of strong fancies and most recently 150-1 Coventry scorer Nando Parrado – and this might be his best shot this year.

The €45,000 yearling made his debut in a hot Newbury 5f maiden in April and was beaten only a neck by the well-backed Hawaiian, with the form franked several times over the next few weeks.

Star Anthem did his bit for the formlines with a four-length victory on his next outing in a considerably easier Bath 5f maiden, making all to put himself in line for a tilt at the Windsor Castle or Norfolk Stakes.

"At the moment five furlongs is far enough and he hits the line well," Cox said. "He ran super at Newbury and the form of that race worked out really well. We like the way he's progressing. I'm pleased we've managed to get two positive runs into him. We'll let him keep his strength now and hopefully he'll be good enough to go to Ascot."

Cox added that Star Anthem had been at home on the Bath ground, which was good to soft as it had been at Newbury. Quicker ground might not be an issue, however, as three of the colt's half-brothers won on good to firm.

'She's pretty special'

SHOOT IT TRUE

This could be the juvenile to put US trainer Wesley Ward back on the scoreboard after he was overshadowed by fellow US trainer George Weaver's Queen Mary success with Crimson Advocate last year.

Shoot It True made an impressive winning debut at Keeneland in early April and still looked Queen Mary-bound despite an odds-on defeat in a stakes race at Churchill Downs four weeks later.

Victory in a 4½f maiden at Keeneland was the starting point for two of Ward's four Queen Mary winners and Shoot It True looked ultra-professional, taking control from the gate and rocketing home by seven and a half lengths.

Her next assignment was more testing against a good field over 5f at Churchill Downs and possibly she lost her chance when she became fractious in the gate. She led into the stretch but faded into fourth.

If Shoot It True doesn't make the trip, Ward has a strong alternative for the Queen Mary in his homebred Saturday Flirt, another 4½f maiden winner at Keeneland in April. She scored by a length and a quarter under Irad Ortiz.

"When Irad got off of her, he told me, 'I just had so much confidence in her and when we turned for home, she took off,'" Ward told The Blood Horse. "For her very first work, we called on Irad. He breezed her from the gate and from that point forward he said, 'This is my filly.'"

Whichever is Ward's filly for the Queen Mary, punters should take note.

RAISE THE BAR

Wesley Ward's top juvenile colt for Royal Ascot looked to be Raise The Bar after his typical prep of a Keeneland 4½f maiden win.

Drawn on the rail, he jumped smartly and was confidently ridden

throughout by John Velazquez to come home in front by a comfortable two and a quarter lengths.

The first of Ward's dozen Royal Ascot winners was Strike The Tiger in the 2009 Windsor Castle Stakes – ridden by Velazquez – and Wednesday's 5f closing race could be the target for Raise The Bar.

MISS RASCAL

"Pretty special" was joint-trainer Oliver Cole's description of Miss Rascal after her easy victory in a 5f fillies' maiden at Ascot, which booked her ticket for a return visit over course and distance in the Queen Mary Stakes.

The daughter of Havana Gold was a major eyecatcher on her debut at Newmarket,

finishing strongly in sixth after blowing the start, and made good on that promise at Ascot with an all-the-way three-length win under Tom Marquand.

Cole, whose fellow joint-trainer and father Paul won the Queen Mary in 1996 with Dance Parade, also has high hopes for juvenile colt Arran – a Newmarket 5f novice winner – but Miss Rascal could be their number one.

"She was unlucky not to win at Newmarket. She got left in the stalls and had to make up seven lengths but got beaten two and three-quarter lengths," he told Sky Sports Racing.

"She's always gone very well at home. I think she's pretty special. She's a typical Havana Gold, quite strong

and compact, and has grown up a lot. I think she'll get further but the jockey recommended five furlongs, so it's the sensible thing to do."

FAIRY GODMOTHER

Having failed to shine on her debut in April, Fairy Godmother produced a much more polished display second time out.

The Aidan O'Brien-trained filly beat four winners – including Sparkling Sea, her debut conqueror – in the often informative Group 3 Fillies Sprint Stakes at Naas on May 19.

The 6f contest is a major stepping stone to the Albany Stakes and the past two winners – Meditate and Porta Fortuna – both went on to land the Friday fillies' race at Royal Ascot. Star miler Alpha Centauri – who was beaten a neck in the Albany – is also on the recent roll of honour.

Fairy Godmother turned a two-and-a-half-length deficit into a neck advantage over Sparkling Sea on their second meeting.

In between the two races, the ante-post market had continued to indicate Fairy Godmother is highly regarded and another step forward will be expected.

Miss Rascal (left): all-the-way Ascot winner second time out

'A real two-year-old'

ANDESITE

The Karl Burke-trained Andesite arrived at York's May meeting with excellent credentials and left with his reputation enhanced after a debut success in a strong-looking 6f novice.

He became the first winner on the track for Pinatubo – a Royal Ascot winner in his champion juvenile season and now an exciting first-season sire – and his pedigree for the royal meeting is deepened by the fact his half-sister Dramatised won the Queen Mary Stakes in the same Clipper Logistics colours two years ago.

Yah Mo Be There led a furlong out but was challenged by Andesite and the pair drew well clear as they engaged in a nip-and-tuck battle. Close home Andesite just got up to score by a short head.

The Coventry looks the likely target for the winner, who was given a smart Racing Post Rating of 90.

The runner-up, whose trainer Richard Spencer won the 2017 Coventry with Rajasinghe, also looks worthy of a place, having run green and suggested there will be improvement to come.

BETTY CLOVER

The Marygate Fillies' Stakes at York's May meeting is a key early test in the north but this year the 5f contest went to Betty Clover from the southern stable of Eve Johnson Houghton.

Remarkably the trainer is also the breeder and owner of the grey daughter of Time Test, who won at Bath on her debut but was then beaten by Running Queen at Salisbury.

At York, though, the filly had that rival almost two lengths back in third as she scored by half a length from Miss Lamai.

Johnson Houghton, who won the Windsor Castle Stakes with Chipotle three years ago, said she was "wildly excited" at the win.

"We have to look at Ascot," she said. "I don't know which race. It's a very fast five furlongs at York and she travelled all right into it, but we'll have a think."

THE ACTOR

Denied by a neck on his debut, winner by a neck second time out. The Actor is closely tied to some of the better juvenile formlines and may just be the one to bring them together in Royal Ascot victory.

The Richard Hannon-trained colt was out early in a 5f novice at Newmarket's Craven meeting in mid-April and was relatively unfancied, going off fifth choice in the betting at 12-1 in a field of six.

He belied his odds, however, with a strong late run that almost overhauled Arran, the 6-1 winner trained by Paul and Oliver Cole.

It was a promising performance, especially with Arran rated a decent shot at the royal meeting for the father-and-son team.

The Actor went into another hot-looking novice over the same course and distance at the Guineas meeting and this time his finishing effort carried him to a narrow victory over Tropical Storm, perhaps the best of Andrew Balding's early juveniles.

Those strong finishes suggested the possibility of a step up in trip, as did the fact his dam won over 1m2f, but the son of star sprinter Harry Angel also showed plenty of speed.

"A tough little horse and a real two-year-old," was how his trainer described him. He could be a real player at Royal Ascot.

Betty Clover: Marygate winner for Eve Johnson Houghton

TROPICAL STORM

The Andrew Balding-trained Tropical Storm was beaten in his first two runs but still he was one of the early high achievers on Racing Post Ratings.

The 50,000gns son of Eqtidaar is one of a pair of juveniles sent to Balding this year by Teme Valley Racing, who are new to the Kingsclere yard but not to Royal Ascot success, having struck to notable effect with

Prince of Wales's Stakes winner State Of Rest in 2022.

Balding might well make an early mark for the burgeoning outfit. Tropical Storm was a promising fifth in a hot 5f maiden at Newbury's April meeting and then was just caught close home by The Actor in a 5f novice on 1,000 Guineas day at Newmarket.

The improvement from his first run was the best part of

a stone on Racing Post Ratings, reaching a high mark of 91 at Newmarket. With the form of both races working out well, that marked out Tropical Storm as a colt with Royal Ascot potential.

Yet perhaps those less than perfect form figures will bring him in slightly under the radar.

Sprinters to the fore

BARELY a year passes now without a Royal Ascot winner from outside Europe and the latest addition to the honours board came in last year's Queen Mary Stakes with Crimson Advocate, trained in the United States by George Weaver.

That was an instant reward for Royal Ascot's initiative in setting up US automatic qualifiers, with the winners of two juvenile five-furlong turf races at Gulfstream Park in May given entry into one of the six two-year-old races at the royal meeting.

One of the Gulfstream winners was Crimson Advocate and her Queen Mary success put Weaver's name up in lights alongside Wesley Ward, who pioneered the art of sending juvenile raiders from the US to the royal meeting. Ward has four Queen Mary winners among his haul of 12 Royal Ascot triumphs since 2009.

An indirect benefit of the US automatic qualifiers is that more American success raises interest in Royal Ascot among other trainers and owners. Chad Brown is set to be a first-time raider this year with Sweet Rebecca, who is entered for the Group 1 Coronation Stakes after her Listed victory at

Aqueduct in April, while John Sadler has put Missed The Cut in the Group 2 Hardwicke Stakes.

Australia is the other main angle of attack from outside Europe and their sprinters have snared seven Group 1 prizes since Choisir's ground-breaking double in 2003 started the international wave of success.

The most famous Australian winner was Black Caviar in the 2012 Diamond Jubilee Stakes and the great mare's trainer Peter Moody has lined up another crack at the race – now called the Queen Elizabeth II Jubilee Stakes – with Group 1 winner Chain Of Lightning.

Moody, now training in partnership with Katherine

WINNERS FROM OUTSIDE GB & IRE SINCE 2000

- France 23
- US 14
- Australia 7
- Hong Kong 2
- Germany 1
- Spain 1

Coleman, stressed two points about Chain Of Lightning when the entries came out: she does not have Black Caviar's class (as he said, "not too many have") and her participation would be dependent on the ownership position after her planned appearance in a mares' sale on May 24.

The other Australian sprint hope is Asfoora in the King Charles III and the mare's trainer Henry Dwyer set out his stall by flying her to Newmarket in late April with the intention of giving her a prep run in the Group 2 Temple Stakes at Haydock on May 25.

Four Japanese-trained entries was an exciting development for Royal Ascot this year. Japan has had Group 1 success in Britain – going back as far as 2000 when Agnes World won the July Cup – and at major international meetings such as the Dubai World Cup and Breeders' Cup, but as yet there has been no Royal Ascot breakthrough.

The interest may not be followed through this year, but the royal meeting certainly seems to have been noted on calendars in Japan – as it is in so many racing jurisdictions.

Year	Horse	Trainer	Country	Race
2003	Choisir	Paul Perry	AUSTRALIA	King's Stand Stakes
	Choisir	Paul Perry	AUSTRALIA	Golden Jubilee Stakes
2005	Cape Of Good Hope	David Oughton	HONG KONG	Golden Jubilee Stakes
2006	Takeover Target	Joe Janiak	AUSTRALIA	King's Stand Stakes
2007	Miss Andretti	Lee Freedman	AUSTRALIA	King's Stand Stakes
2009	Scenic Blast	Daniel Morton	AUSTRALIA	King's Stand Stakes
	Strike The Tiger	Wesley Ward	USA	Windsor Castle Stakes
	Jealous Again	Wesley Ward	USA	Queen Mary Stakes
2012	Little Bridge	Danny Shum	HONG KONG	King's Stand Stakes
	Black Caviar	Peter Moody	AUSTRALIA	Diamond Jubilee Stakes
2013	No Nay Never	Wesley Ward	USA	Norfolk Stakes
2014	Hootenanny	Wesley Ward	USA	Windsor Castle Stakes
2015	Acapulco	Wesley Ward	USA	Queen Mary Stakes
	Undrafted	Wesley Ward	USA	Diamond Jubilee Stakes
2016	Tepin	Mark Casse	USA	Queen Anne Stakes
	Lady Aurelia	Wesley Ward	USA	Queen Mary Stakes
2017	Lady Aurelia	Wesley Ward	USA	King's Stand Stakes
	Con Te Partiro	Wesley Ward	USA	Sandringham Handicap
2018	Shang Shang Shang	Wesley Ward	USA	Norfolk Stakes
2020	Campanelle	Wesley Ward	USA	Queen Mary Stakes
2021	Campanelle	Wesley Ward	USA	Commonwealth Cup
2022	Nature Strip	Chris Waller	AUSTRALIA	King's Stand Stakes
2023	Crimson Advocate	George Weaver	USA	Queen Mary Stakes

Crimson Advocate (red): fifth US-trained Queen Mary Stakes winner

SINCE 2003, 220 RUNNERS FROM OUTSIDE EUROPE HAVE COMPETED AT ROYAL ASCOT FROM TEN JURISDICTIONS: USA, AUSTRALIA, NEW ZEALAND, JAPAN, SINGAPORE, HONG KONG, SOUTH AFRICA, BAHRAIN, UAE AND QATAR

King of the world

BIG ROCK produced one of the best performances at Ascot last year even without appearing at the royal meeting. His signature display was a six-length win in the Queen Elizabeth II Stakes on Champions Day that earned him the title of world champion miler in 2023.

The French-trained colt's official rating of 127 – bettered at Ascot only by Mostahdaf's 128 in the Prince of Wales's Stakes – will make him the one to beat if he lines up for the Queen Anne Stakes in the opening race of Royal Ascot 2024.

There has been seismic change since the QEII, however. In late April, Big Rock was moved by Yeguada Centurion, the ownership and breeding entity of Spanish-based Leopoldo Fernandez Pujals, from Christopher Head's yard across Chantilly to Maurizio Guarnieri. He was one of 33 horses – also including dual Classic-winning filly Blue Rose Cen – to make the shock switch.

The pressure is on Guarnieri to maintain the high standards set by Head with the Yeguada Centurion stars, in particular Big Rock, and things did not go well on the champion's reappearance in the Lockinge Stakes at Newbury.

In a thoroughly unsatisfactory race, front-runner Audience stole a march on the field and Big Rock was among the stragglers, trailing in 15 lengths adrift in sixth place.

Perhaps it's a race to write off when put alongside last year's excellent form.

The jaw-dropping QEII demolition came on soft

ground in late season but there was always a sense that the son of Rock Of Gibraltar was capable of something special as a three-year-old.

He went off favourite for the Prix du Jockey Club, where he was beaten only by subsequent Arc winner Ace Impact, and on his return to a mile he went close in the Prix Jacques le Marois behind Inspiral and the Prix du Moulin behind Sauterne.

More testing ground in the QEII was a key factor and he poured on the power from the front under Aurelien Lemaitre,

keeping up what appeared to be an unsustainable pace to go well clear of Facteur Cheval and Tahiyra.

The big questions, then, are whether Big Rock will get his preferred ground in

midsummer – he has yet to win without soft or heavy in the description – and whether Guarnieri can produce him at the same level only a few weeks after the yard switch and the Lockinge defeat.

Positive answers could produce something special again.

STAR RATING
★ ★ ★ ★ ★

Big Rock: huge impact at Ascot in last year's QEII

FACTEUR CHEVAL knocked on the door in Group 1 races last season without quite delivering, but he was quick to stamp himself a top-level winner this year with the promise of more to come.

Unraced at two and a Group 3 winner at three, the Jerome Reynier-trained gelding finally made it into the elite late in May of his four-year-old campaign. From there the upwardly mobile miler finished 3232 in consecutive Group 1s, two at Longchamp and the others at Goodwood and Ascot.

Success finally arrived in the Dubai Turf on World Cup night at Meydan in March when Facteur Cheval overcame a Group 1 field of the highest quality.

The short-head runner-up was Namur, whose previous two runs had brought victory in the Group 1 Mile Championship back home in Japan and third place in the Hong Kong Mile. Danon Beluga, the previous year's Dubai Turf runner-up, was third, and fourth was Godolphin's recent Group 1 winner Measured Time.

Further back were European luminaries Lord North (who was going for a fourth Dubai Turf in a row), Nashwa and Luxembourg.

That race was over 1m1f, the same trip over which Facteur Cheval finished a

Major factor

close third in last year's Prix d'Ispahan on his first attempt in Group 1 company, but the plan is to take him back to his usual mile in the Queen Anne Stakes at Royal Ascot rather than up another step for the Prince of Wales's Stakes.

"He really needs a race where they go a good gallop in order for him to get into a rhythm that brings out the best in him," Reynier said. "The issue in stepping him up in trip is the risk that won't be the case, even if there is usually pace on at Royal Ascot.

"He performed so well up the straight mile in the QEII that I think we could have a

Facteur Cheval (right): high-quality win in the Dubai Turf

crack at the Queen Anne without any problem."

Facteur Cheval was a well-beaten six lengths behind Big Rock in the Queen Elizabeth II on Champions Day, which came on the soft ground that up to then had brought out his best form, including second place behind

Paddington in the Sussex Stakes.

The Dubai Turf was run on good ground, however, and that increases the scope for Reynier. "We didn't know if he would be competitive on quicker ground, but the best horse won," he said in the Meydan winner's enclosure.

With Reynier's hand

slightly forced by the paucity of top mile and ten-furlong races open to geldings in France, Facteur Cheval is set to be a frequent visitor to Britain again. His Group 1 form figures indicate he will be a major factor every time.

STAR RATING
★★★★

137

Rouhiya

Owner: HH The Aga Khan
Trainer: Francis Graffard

Rapid progress

ROUHIYA flourished fast in the spring and she finished fast at Longchamp to score a home win in the Poule d'Essai des Pouliches. That set up the exciting possibility of an away trip to Britain in the Coronation Stakes.

Classic success had looked unlikely for the Aga Khan homebred, hence Rouhiya's odds of 31-1. Trainer Francis Graffard faced a race against time to give her a prep and eventually had to run her in a conditions race on heavy ground just over three weeks before France's 1,000 Guineas.

Third place did not look that promising but Rouhiya thrived afterwards, as Graffard reported.

"It took a long time to get her out this season because she's a real good-ground filly," he said. "But she came on a bundle for the run. Princess Zahra [Aga Khan] said to me that there's only one Poule d'Essai and that we should try our luck. It's my first Group 1 for the Aga Khan and it's a Classic, with a filly I've always loved."

The Pouliches was only the fourth outing for Rouhiya, which raises hope for more improvement to come. She was third on her turf debut last October and signed off her short juvenile campaign

Rouhiya: Pouliches winner is "a real good-ground filly"

with victory in a minor conditions race on the Deauville all-weather.

"When she won at Deauville I knew she must be good because of the way she finished," said Graffard. The way she finished at Longchamp was even better.

The famous Aga Khan colours were carried to Coronation victory last year by Tahiyra, whose spring also featured Guineas success in the Irish 1,000. Rouhiya has some way to go to match her fellow homebred, however.

Her Guineas-winning Racing Post Rating was 108, whereas Tahiyra's was 115 (and she had already twice gone above that mark). Yet there was distinct promise in the rapid turn of pace Rouhiya showed to claim Classic victory once an opening appeared.

As Princess Zahra said: "When they have that acceleration over a mile, you can always hope."

STAR RATING
★★★★

Unfinished business

BLUE ROSE CEN'S first trip to Britain didn't go as planned. It left the feeling of unfinished business and a return visit looks on the cards this year. There could be no better venue than Royal Ascot.

The four-year-old filly could make the journey with Big Rock from the Chantilly yard of Maurizio Guarnieri, who has taken over the training of both luminaries this year following owner Leopoldo Fernandez Pujals' split with Christopher Head.

For her former trainer, Blue Rose Cen won France's 1,000 Guineas and Oaks last season. With her reputation sky high, she headed to Glorious Goodwood as odds-on favourite for the Nassau Stakes but was a disappointing fourth after a troubled passage.

Another defeat followed back home over 1m4f before she recovered her form back at 1m2f with Group 1 victory in the Prix de l'Opera on Arc day at Longchamp. It came with soft in the going description, just like her Classic wins and her Group 1 success as a juvenile.

The Prince of Wales's Stakes looks a natural target for a four-year-old of her quality kept in training, although it would ask a question that was never put to her last season: can she beat male rivals?

All six of her runs in 2023 were against her own sex and she reached a peak in the Prix de Diane with a Racing Post Rating of 118. She will have to step up to mix it with the best in open company but the fact that the Breeders' Cup came under serious consideration at the end of last season was a sign that there is no concern about travelling her to more top races.

The chance for her to show what she can really do in Britain would be relished.

STAR RATING
★★★★

Blue Rose Cen: soft in the going description for all four Group 1 wins

139

Classic stormer

BY THE time the fourth major Guineas had been run in May, the winners had been returned at 16-1, 28-1, 31-1 and 24-1. It was a spring of upsets.

Metropolitan, who completed that sequence in the Poule d'Essai des Poulains, was such a surprising winner that he was the only one of the four without a Royal Ascot entry. It was an omission his connections were minded to put right after his step up to the top level.

"I don't really want to stretch him out and, although he's not entered in the St James's Palace, we could look at supplementing him." said trainer Mario Baratti, the Chantilly-based Italian who claimed his first Group 1 success in the Poulains.

Metropolitan's victory was enveloped in drama. A huge electrical storm hit Longchamp before the race and the runners were sent from the paddock back to the stables as torrential rain and hail lashed the track.

When the race got under way after a 35-minute delay, Alexis Pouchin aboard Metropolitan had a dream run on the inner from stall one while others – notably favourite Henry Longfellow

– ran into trouble further back.

The pre-race downpour had fallen on already soft ground – the winning time was 1.85sec slower than the preceding fillies' mile Classic – and the bunched finish raised further doubts.

The first four were covered by a length, with Metropolitan given a Racing Post Rating of 114 for his half-length win over Dancing Gemini.

Winner of both starts as a juvenile over a mile, Metropolitan had been fifth of six on his return in the Prix de Fontainebleau, which did not look an inspiring trial for the Poulains.

Yet, with the doubts about the form, Pouchin gave an upbeat assessment of Metropolitan. "He had a nice quiet comeback and didn't run all that badly if you watched it closely," he said. "He's a very good horse. He has a turn of foot that all the good horses have; not a real kick, but he accelerates and then keeps going."

The jockey's faith is worth bearing in mind, although many will take more convincing of Metropolitan's true merit.

STAR RATING
★★★

66Although he's not entered in the St James's Palace, we could look at supplementing him**99**

Metropolitan: dream run on the inner to win the French 2,000 Guineas

Moody in the hunt again

CHAIN OF LIGHTNING is no Black Caviar, that's for sure, even if she is a Group 1-winning sprint mare from Australia trained by Peter Moody. There is no doubt, however, that she is capable of a strong showing in the Queen Elizabeth II Jubilee Stakes on the final day of Royal Ascot.

A dozen years have passed since Black Caviar's heart-stopping victory for Moody in the same race, then known as the Diamond Jubilee Stakes. That was just one of 15 Group 1 triumphs in a glittering 25-race unbeaten career for Australia's greatest sprint mare.

By contrast, Chain Of Lightning has managed only one Group 1 win by the age of five in 23 outings. It came recently in the TJ Smith Stakes at Randwick on April 6, although the result could easily have gone differently in a blanket finish where the first seven were covered by just a length.

In fact, placings were firmly reversed a fortnight later when TJ Smith seventh Magic Time stepped up to take the Group 1 All Aged Stakes over Randwick's seven furlongs, with Chain Of Lightning back in sixth. Heavy ground compromised her chance there – it was soft for the TJ Smith – and her earlier win may be the stronger formline.

Moody, who now trains in partnership with former assistant Katherine Coleman, reckons there could be more to come in British conditions.

"She's a strong, robust mare who's pretty bombproof," he said. "She appreciates a little bit of cut in the ground and her form in recent seasons has been curtailed by very firm tracks. Firm by our standards is very firm by British standards, so I think she'll appreciate the surface at Ascot, and she's very good over seven furlongs, which in my opinion is what you need to win over the 1,200m there."

Chain Of Lightning's participation was set to be decided after her appearance in a mares' sale in late May but Moody believes she merits a crack, even if she would not arrive with the same level of expectation as Black Caviar.

"She's not as big as Black Caviar, but there's certainly plenty of size and strength about her," he said. "She doesn't have the class of a Black Caviar, not too many have, but under the right conditions I think she can be competitive anywhere."

Owner: Ramsay Pastoral Pty Ltd
Trainers: Peter Moody & Katherine Coleman

> **"I think she'll appreciate the surface at Ascot, and she's very good over seven furlongs"**

Chain Of Lightning: "Strong, robust and pretty bombproof"

Reflecting on Black Caviar's win, he added: "It's quite extraordinary that it was 12 years ago. Because I'd been over a couple of times before, it was nice to get that success. We were gutted a year earlier when we brought Hinchinbrook and he went amiss on the eve of the race. I think Chain Of Lightning sits in the mould of a Hinchinbrook or a Magnus, who was third in the King's Stand, in terms of quality."

Magnus ran to a Racing Post Rating of 120 when he was third to Australia's Miss Andretti in the 2007 King's Stand, while Chain Of Lightning reached a peak of 119 in the TJ Smith. She's in the right ballpark to be competitive.

STAR RATING
★★★

143

Sweet promise

THE United States has had two Coronation Stakes runners-up in the past four runnings, which suggests Sweet Rebecca merits some respect if she makes the trip even if she is a big price.

The daughter of American Pharoah is set to be a first Royal Ascot runner for four-time Eclipse Award winner Chad Brown, who said the Coronation would be her next stop after she won a Listed mile race at Aqueduct in late April.

That was only her second start and her first for Brown following her purchase by ambitious owner-breeder John Stewart's Resolute Racing. Stewart burst on to the scene at the breeding stock sales last autumn, purchasing a number of multi-million-dollar broodmares, and he moved quickly to purchase Sweet Rebecca privately after her winning debut in a maiden at Gulfstream Park in March.

She was quite green at Gulfstream but much more professional on her second start, settling well and gliding along the rail under Tyler Gaffalione before scoring by a length and a half.

Brown said: "It all worked out and I think this filly might be my first Ascot starter. For right now, I'd say it's likely her next start would

be in the Coronation. She's a serious filly and trains with a lot of power.

"I want to thank Mr Stewart for purchasing her and transferring her to me and my team. He's new in the game and building an impressive roster of racehorses and broodmares."

Stewart is a fan of American Pharoah as a broodmare sire and Sweet Rebecca is a sister to three-time Graded winner Sweet Melania, who was third in the 2019 Breeders' Cup Juvenile Fillies Turf.

Coincidentally, the winner of that Breeders' Cup race was Sharing, who went on to be runner-up in the Coronation the following year. Two years later her trainer Graham Motion returned to finish second again with Spendarella.

Sweet Rebecca is not at the level of those American challengers after just two starts but is an interesting contender for her ambitious owner.

Her turn of foot in the final quarter-mile was impressive on her debut, especially given how headstrong she had been early in the race, and her improvement from there to her second start bodes well for more progress at Royal Ascot.

STAR RATING
★★★

Spendarella (right): the most recent US-trained filly to run well in the Coronation when second to Inspiral in 2022

Long-range planning

AUSTRALIAN raiders have enjoyed most success in the King Charles III Stakes – five wins from 2003 to 2022 under its former name of the King's Stand – and Asfoora is set to be their latest representative in the fastest race of the week.

The five-year-old mare is trained by Henry Dwyer, a rising star of the Melbourne scene who has enjoyed multiple Group 1 wins even if he has yet to notch one with Asfoora.

Her best performance was last October's victory in the Group 2 Schillaci Stakes over five and a half furlongs at Caulfield, earning a Racing Post Rating of 121. That was preceded by a high-class effort in top-level company at Moonee Valley when she was beaten just over a length in second behind Imperatriz, the world's second-best turf sprinter before her retirement in April.

The Moonee Valley race was over six furlongs and it was the opportunity to run the speedy Asfoora over shorter that prompted Dwyer to look towards Royal Ascot and other British targets.

"She's not the easiest to place in that she's one of our better sprinters in Australia – not the best by any means but in the top ten," the trainer said. "However, most of our best sprints are over 1,200m, whereas in Britain there's a good programme over 1,000m at Haydock, Ascot, Goodwood and York, which is why we decided to travel."

The testing five furlongs – or 1,000m in Australian parlance – should be ideal in the King Charles III, according to Dwyer.

"Her last three wins have come over 1,100m, but she has form over 1,200m and everyone tells me the King Charles III Stakes rides more like a six-furlong race," he said.

"It won't be an easy task for her, although it's all relative to the competition. We have bumped into Imperatriz a couple of times and, if we can be semi-competitive with her, we're hoping that'll translate to Britain."

Asfoora has been based in Newmarket since late April with the aim of a prep run in the Group 2 Temple Stakes at Haydock before heading on to her royal date.

Dwyer said: "It's very exciting to be bringing a runner to Royal Ascot. I've been to the meeting three or four times and it's always a lovely experience. To have a runner there has long been an ambition of mine and hopefully Asfoora can tick that box well."

STAR RATING
★★★

Asfoora during track gallops at Moonee Valley racecourse

American wildcard

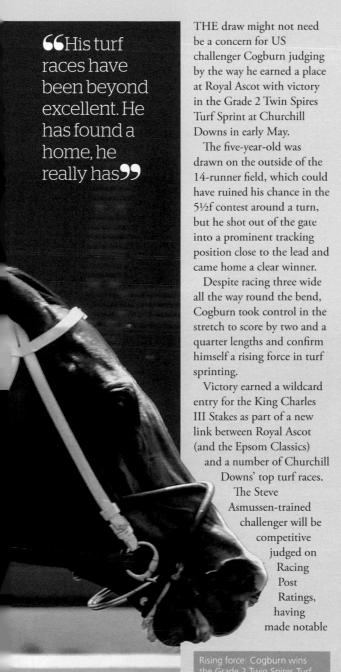

> **"His turf races have been beyond excellent. He has found a home, he really has"**

THE draw might not need be a concern for US challenger Cogburn judging by the way he earned a place at Royal Ascot with victory in the Grade 2 Twin Spires Turf Sprint at Churchill Downs in early May.

The five-year-old was drawn on the outside of the 14-runner field, which could have ruined his chance in the 5½f contest around a turn, but he shot out of the gate into a prominent tracking position close to the lead and came home a clear winner.

Despite racing three wide all the way round the bend, Cogburn took control in the stretch to score by two and a quarter lengths and confirm himself a rising force in turf sprinting.

Victory earned a wildcard entry for the King Charles III Stakes as part of a new link between Royal Ascot (and the Epsom Classics) and a number of Churchill Downs' top turf races. The Steve Asmussen-trained challenger will be competitive judged on Racing Post Ratings, having made notable progress since being switched to turf sprinting in April last year.

He was a fairly ordinary dirt performer, winning three of his eight starts but managing only one Grade 3 placing. By contrast, he has won four out of five in his new discipline, including a Grade 3 victory at Saratoga last summer when he beat subsequent Breeders' Cup Turf Sprint winner Nobals by three-quarters of a length.

The Saratoga win, also over 5½f, was all the more impressive given a troubled start where he was involved in a couple of bumps. Cogburn's polished start on his reappearance at Churchill Downs was a sign of further improvement.

"The good start hasn't been typical for him but then he broke so well," Asmussen told The Blood Horse after the Twin Spires win. "His turf races have been beyond excellent. He has found a home, he really has."

Asmussen has set the Breeders' Cup Turf Sprint as the long-term goal and it looks a realistic ambition given the form tie-in with last year's winner.

Royal Ascot is more of a punt but one well worth taking after Cogburn's recent progress.

Rising force: Cogburn wins the Grade 2 Twin Spires Turf Sprint at Churchill Downs

STAR RATING
★★★

Distance question

THE result of the 1,000 Guineas at Newmarket left Ramatuelle's connections with a familiar dilemma: stay at a mile in a bid for Royal Ascot glory in the Coronation Stakes or drop back to sprinting in the Commonwealth Cup?

It is a question that has been faced many times in the decade since the introduction of the Group 1 sprint for three-year-olds – not only with fillies coming out of a mile Classic but also with colts potentially heading to the St James's Palace Stakes.

In Ramatuelle's case, there were complicating factors with her run at Newmarket. Often it is obvious whether the mile has been well and truly stayed, but not for the Christopher Head-trained filly.

Aurelien Lemaitre was widely criticised for going too soon on Ramatuelle, who was trying a mile for the first time and has never won beyond 6f. She took the lead heading into the Dip with more than two furlongs to run but was caught close

Ramatuelle (no.8): edged out close home in the 1,000 Guineas

home by Elmalka and Porta Fortuna, losing out by a neck and a short head.

There were plenty who thought the French filly would have won with a better-timed ride, although she wasn't the only one with a claim as moral winner of the 1,000 Guineas (fourth-placed Tamfana was notably unlucky in running).

Head felt the race would settle whether Ramatuelle stayed a mile, given that her trial in the 7f Prix Imprudence had been slowly run and offered no real pointer. In the event, the waters were muddied further.

A mile programme has long been set for her – looking at France as well as Britain – and sticking to that plan would make a lot of sense until there is strong counter-evidence.

Yet there is no doubt her sprinting credentials are well established on pedigree and form. Last season she won the Group 2 Prix Robert Papin by four lengths and was beaten just a short neck in the Group 1 Prix Morny by Vandeek, who later added the Middle Park Stakes and is a leading prospect for the sprint crown.

Wherever Ramatuelle turns up, much of the spotlight will be on Lemaitre, who has yet to win at Royal Ascot but excelled at the track with his front-running victory on Big Rock for Head in the Queen Elizabeth II Stakes on Champions Day last October.

With that exceptional miler having left the yard over the winter, Ramatuelle offers a path back to the Ascot big time for her yard.

STAR RATING
★★★★

Record breaker

THE O'Brien name was spread across the Royal Ascot honours board last year with four wins for Aidan, two for eldest son Joseph and a first at the meeting for Donnacha, his other training son.

It was the family patriarch who set the standard not just for his sons but everyone else too. He tied on wins with John and Thady Gosden but beat them easily on places (six seconds to their one) to claim a 12th trainers' title at Royal Ascot.

His opening-day double with River Tiber (Coventry Stakes) and Paddington (St James's Palace Stakes) took him past Sir Michael Stoute as the meeting's all-time record trainer and further wins with Warm Heart (Ribblesdale Stakes) and Age Of Kings (Jersey Stakes) left him three clear at the top with a total of 85.

Only one of last year's winners went off favourite (River Tiber at 11-8) but Paddington was 11-5 second favourite and Warm Heart third at 13-2. That reinforced the trend for O'Brien's best chances to be well indicated in the market. Fourteen of his 20 winners (70%) in the past five years have been no bigger than 5-1 and ten were favourite.

He has the occasional big-priced winner (Age Of Kings was 22-1 last year and so was South Pacific in the King George V Handicap in 2019) and the best place to find one is in a race restricted to a single age group – two-year-olds or three-year-olds.

All nine of his winners in the past decade priced in double figures fitted that criterion and it wasn't such a surprise that last year's big-priced win came in the Jersey Stakes, given how well stocked he is with three-year-olds who may not have made the top

85
ROYAL ASCOT WINNERS

12
TOP TRAINER AWARDS

grade in miling or sprinting.

From 16 Jersey runners in the past decade, he has had a winner (22-1), two seconds (one at 66-1) and two thirds (one at 14-1).

Four of the nine double-figure winners in the past decade came in juvenile races, including the Norfolk Stakes on two occasions (Waterloo Bridge at 12-1 and Sioux Nation at 14-1) when the winner was the stable's only representative and was ridden by Ryan Moore.

O'Brien has had 11 runners in the Norfolk in the past decade, mostly one a year, and apart from the two winners he has had a third and three fourths.

Moore is worth noting when he has a handicap ride for O'Brien. The trainer has had three winners from 37 runners in that sphere since 2015 and it is notable that two were the only runners in their respective races and were ridden by Moore, returning SPs of 7-1 and 10-1. Moore had just 22 rides in handicaps for O'Brien in that timeframe, with four others finishing second at 7-1, 11-2, 4-1 and 2-1.

1997
YEAR OF FIRST
ROYAL ASCOT
WINNER

O'BRIEN'S ROYAL ASCOT WINNERS BY AGE GROUP

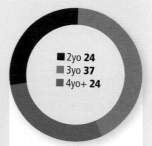

- 2yo **24**
- 3yo **37**
- 4yo+ **24**

MOST SUCCESSFUL RACES

Coventry Stakes
▪▪▪▪▪▪▪▪▪▪

St James's Palace Stakes
▪▪▪▪▪▪▪▪▪

Gold Cup
▪▪▪▪▪▪▪▪

Queen's Vase
▪▪▪▪▪▪▪

Chesham Stakes
▪▪▪▪▪▪

Hampton Court Stakes
▪▪▪▪

Hardwicke Stakes
▪▪▪▪

Jersey Stakes
▪▪▪▪

Prince of Wales's Stakes
▪▪▪▪

Queen Anne Stakes
▪▪▪▪

Ribblesdale Stakes
▪▪▪▪

Coronation Stakes
▪▪▪

King Edward VII Stakes
▪▪▪

Norfolk Stakes
▪▪▪

Windsor Castle Stakes
▪▪▪

The Group races for middle-distance/staying types are a strong point. In the past decade he has had four winners in the Ribblesdale Stakes, three in the Queen's Vase and two apiece in the Hardwicke Stakes and King Edward VII Stakes. He had 14 runners-up in those four Group 2 races alone in the past decade, emphasising his competitiveness.

Continued success

THREE Royal Ascots for the Gosden father-and-son team have brought win totals of four, one and four and the leading trainer award in 2021, which is much in line with the Clarehaven stable's high level of success since 2012.

Last year's four wins almost brought another award but they were beaten on number of places by Aidan O'Brien. Overall the Gosden stable is second only to O'Brien at the past five meetings, with 17 winners to Ballydoyle's 20 in that time (next after the Gosdens is Roger Varian on ten).

Their big winners in 2023 were Mostahdaf in the Prince of Wales's Stakes and Courage Mon Ami in the Gold Cup, along with Gregory (Queen's Vase) and Coppice (Sandringham Handicap).

Given that the Gosdens have plenty of runners, the key for punters is to find ways of narrowing the focus.

One angle is that the record with fancied runners is pretty good. In the past decade, 19 of the Gosdens' 31 winners have been priced at 6-1 or below, from 77 runners in that category. The win percentage is 25%.

It is worth noting that seven of the other 12 Gosden winners since 2014 were priced at 8-1 to 12-1 (and all in that price bracket were in the first six in the betting market), emphasising that it is rare for them to win with an outsider.

Handicap favourites are well worth watching, as three of the stable's five winners in that sphere in the past decade headed the market (and another was second favourite). The yard had 12 handicap favourites in that period, which works out at a 25% strike-rate (two others went close in second place).

Gosden snr has long been known for his patient handling of horses and it is often a good sign when the stable has a two-year-old ready to run at the meeting. From just 23 juvenile runners in the past decade, three won at odds of 10-1, 20-1 and 2-1 (13%, +12pts).

MOST SUCCESSFUL RACES

Prince of Wales's Stakes
■■■■■
Ribblesdale Stakes
■■■■■
Britannia Handicap
■■■■
Gold Cup
■■■■
Wolferton Stakes
■■■■
Chesham Stakes
■■■
Coronation Stakes
■■■
Duke of Cambridge Stakes
■■■
King Edward VII Stakes
■■■
Queen's Vase
■■■
St James's Palace Stakes
■■■

64

ROYAL ASCOT WINNERS

3

TOP TRAINER AWARDS

1990
YEAR OF FIRST
ROYAL ASCOT
WINNER

GOSDEN ROYAL
ASCOT WINNERS BY
DISTANCE (2012-)

- 5-7f 4
- 1m/1m2f 19
- 1m4f/1m6f 10
- 2m/2m4f 4

*Combined figures for John and Thady Gosden

Bright prospects

THE Godolphin team were winless at Royal Ascot in a difficult 2023 but their prospects are much brighter this year and a return to their usual challenging position is on the cards, especially for principal trainer Charlie Appleby (right).

The Newmarket trainer set the tone with Notable Speech's impressive 2,000 Guineas success and the unbeaten potential superstar looks set to head a strong squad.

Appleby provides the bulk of Godolphin runners and winners nowadays and his score stands at 15 in ten Royal Ascots since he stepped up from his previous job as assistant.

He has yet to take the leading trainer award but has had five Group 1 winners. Four of those were in sprints and the other came over a mile with Coroebus, his previous 2,000 Guineas winner in 2022, who then took the St James's Palace Stakes.

Improving, lightly raced three-year-olds are a core strength. The King Edward VII Stakes, Queen's Vase, Jersey Stakes, Hampton Court Stakes and King George V Handicap all appear on Appleby's honours list at least once. His winners of those races came to Royal Ascot with an average of just over five runs (the highest number was eight) and notably all seven had won last time out.

Saeed bin Suroor, formerly the lead trainer and four times the award winner at Royal Ascot, is still capable of hitting the target despite his reduced string. A late developer in one of the handicaps or a Group 3 looks his most likely type now.

Handicaps can be a fruitful area in general for Godolphin runners, and the Royal Hunt Cup, King George V and Duke of Edinburgh are the three particularly worth focusing on.

Competitive force

SIR MICHAEL STOUTE may no longer be the leading all-time trainer at Royal Ascot after being overtaken last year by Aidan O'Brien but the competitive spirit remains strong.

Evidence of that comes in the proportion of runners each of the top trainers manage to get in the first three. Among those with four or more winners in the past five years, O'Brien unsurprisingly leads with 33.7 per cent of his runners making the first three, but Stoute is a close second with 32.6 per cent.

Stoute's number of runners is much lower and that has an impact on his winners – three at the past five meetings, albeit two of them in Group 1 races. He is still a major force with the right quality – and very possibly he has that with Passenger this year.

Yet the high proportion in the first three makes all Stoute runners well worth a look, especially now that the focus is often elsewhere and the market may not be quite so alive to his chances.

Nowadays, he has come to rely on a handful of races for the bulk of his winners. The Hardwicke Stakes (eight), Duke of Cambridge Stakes (five), Duke of Edinburgh Handicap (four) and King Edward VII Stakes (three) account for more than half of his winners since 2004.

What is notable about those favourite races is that three of the four are run at 1m4f. The exception is the Duke of Cambridge over a mile, although that race is for fillies and mares – a department where Stoute also tends to be well stocked.

Stoute's haul of 11 winners in the Hardwicke is the biggest number recorded by any trainer in the modern era in a Group race at this meeting.

MOST SUCCESSFUL RACES

Hardwicke Stakes
■■■■■■■■■■■

King Edward VII Stakes
■■■■■■■

Duke of Edinburgh Handicap
■■■■■■

Jersey Stakes
■■■■■■

King George V Handicap
■■■■■

Britannia Handicap
■■■■

Coronation Stakes
■■■■

Duke of Cambridge Stakes
■■■■

Prince of Wales's Stakes
■■■■

Queen's Vase
■■■■

Hampton Court Stakes
■■■

Queen Anne Stakes
■■■

Ribblesdale Stakes
■■■

82
ROYAL ASCOT WINNERS

6
TOP TRAINER AWARDS

1977
YEAR OF FIRST ROYAL ASCOT WINNER

Scoreboard regulars

ROGER VARIAN

Two winners last year moved the Newmarket trainer up to third in the recent rankings. With ten winners over the past five meetings, he is behind only Aidan O'Brien and the John and Thady Gosden stable.

Those two operations are also the only ones that can beat Varian for second and third places in that period, which emphasises that he has truly arrived as an elite competitor at Royal Ascot.

All but one of his ten winners at the last five meetings were 8-1 or shorter and six went off favourite (including King Of Steel at 11-10 in the King Edward VII Stakes last year). His record with favourites since 2019 is 111121001.

The only longer-priced success was his other winner last year, Royal Champion at 16-1 in the Wolferton Stakes.

Note his runners in the Hardwicke and Ribblesdale, plus handicaps such as the Buckingham Palace, Copper Horse, Palace of Holyroodhouse, Kensington Palace and Duke of Edinburgh.

ANDREW BALDING

The Kingsclere trainer missed out at Royal Ascot last year after hitting the scoreboard at four consecutive meetings but three second places – as many as anyone apart from Aidan O'Brien – were a good sign that a return to the winner's enclosure can be expected.

Two of the seconds came in prestige events with Chaldean in the St James's Palace Stakes and Coltrane in the Gold Cup, with the other being Queen's Vase runner-up Saint George.

Even so, eight winners at the past five meetings put Balding fifth in that period.

He is strong across the board, with three wins in the meeting's heritage handicaps. three at 2m-plus (including the Queen Alexandra Stakes twice) and three in juvenile events (Coventry, Albany and Windsor Castle Stakes).

The market is a good indicator, with five of his eight winners at the last five meetings priced below 10-1.

WILLIAM HAGGAS

The Newmarket trainer had only one winner at last year's meeting but it was one of the most significant. He sent out Desert Hero to land the King George V Handicap for the King and Queen, giving them a first Royal Ascot success.

That took Haggas (below) to 15 in total and seven have come at the last five meetings from 69 runners (10% strike-rate), along with eight seconds, six thirds and eight fourths (42% in the first four). Conditions races below Group 1 over a mile and 1m2f have been a fruitful source in recent years, along with 1m4f handicaps.

WESLEY WARD

Since first taking the meeting by storm in 2009 with a pair of lightning-fast two-year-old winners in Jealous Again (Queen Mary Stakes) and Strike The Tiger (Windsor Castle Stakes), the US trainer has advanced his score to 12. He has had at least one winner at eight of

the last 11 meetings, although two blanks have come in the last two years.

Nine of the 12 wins have been over five furlongs, which suits his fast, precocious horses ideally. The other three have come with more mature runners, two over six furlongs and the other over a mile.

Ward has compiled his enviable record from only 87 runners at a 14 per cent strike-rate. At odds below 7-1, his strike-rate almost doubles to 27 per cent (9-33) for a level-stake profit of 12.5pts, which demonstrates how well focused his team is on winning (five of the others were second).

The bulk of his runners and most of his winners have been in two-year-old races (8-63, 13%, +6pts).

CHARLIE JOHNSTON

The Middleham trainer is looking for his first winner after two Royal Ascots, first as joint-trainer with father Mark in 2022 and last year on his own (albeit with his father as full-time assistant). He had three places last year, going closest with Golden Gates Handicap runner-up Lion Of War.

Johnston snr had 47 Royal Ascot winners and much of the success came in the longer-distance events. The King George V Handicap (1m4f), Queen's Vase (1m6f/2m), Gold Cup (2m4f), Hardwicke Stakes (1m4f), Duke of Edinburgh Handicap (1m4f), King Edward VII Stakes (1m4f) and Queen Alexandra Stakes (2m6f) account for 64 per cent of the Johnston winners.

At the other end of the scale, fancied juveniles are worth a close look. From 17 priced at 10-1 or below in the past decade, the stable has had two winners, two seconds and a third.

WILLIE MULLINS

The Irish and British champion jumps trainer has been on the scoreboard from only a handful of runners at the past three meetings, taking his score to nine from 45 runners (20%) since his breakthrough in 2012.

Until last year all the wins had been in the Queen Alexandra Stakes and the Ascot Handicap and his strike-rate in those two long-distance races since 2012 is 26 per cent (+23.5pts).

Last year's success came in the 1m6f Copper Horse Handicap (he had the one-two with Vauban and Absurde) and that recent addition to the programme is likely to continue as another prime target.

LEADING TRAINERS IN LAST FIVE YEARS

Trainer	Wins	2nds	3rds	Runs
Aidan O'Brien	20	24	13	169
John & Thady Gosden*	17	10	11	140
Roger Varian	10	8	8	89
Charlie Appleby	9	4	12	91
Andrew Balding	8	9	6	128
William Haggas	7	8	6	69
Charlie (& Mark) Johnston*	4	5	10	116
Richard Fahey	4	2	3	59
Charlie Hills	4	2	1	52
Karl Burke	4	0	4	43
Kevin Ryan	4	0	3	36
Sir Michael Stoute	3	7	6	49
Joseph O'Brien	3	5	4	54
Richard Hannon	3	5	0	102
Archie Watson	3	4	4	69
Willie Mullins	3	4	1	17
Ralph Beckett	3	3	4	54
Alan King	3	3	1	18
Charlie Fellowes	3	2	2	29
Jessica Harrington	3	1	2	26

Includes trainers with at least three wins since 2019
*Includes joint and individual figures

Scoreboard regulars

OTHERS TO NOTE

Joseph O'Brien looks set to be a growing force judging by last year's results, which saw him treble his win tally to three (along with two seconds and a third). The same goes for **Archie Watson**, a sprint and two-year-old specialist who took his total to five with three winners last year.

Another likely riser is **Ralph Beckett**, who had one winner last year with Jimi Hendrix in the Royal Hunt Cup (taking him to four overall) but had six finishers in the first three (bettered only by Aidan O'Brien).

The top northern-based trainer is **Richard Fahey** with ten winners, although the best he had last year was a second and a third. Close behind is **Kevin Ryan** (right), who took his score to nine with Triple Time's Queen Anne victory last year. Fahey has also won the big mile Group 1 (with Ribchester in 2017) but most success for the big northern stables comes below that distance – eight out of ten for Fahey, seven out of nine for Ryan and all five for **Karl Burke** (also winless last year but in

contention with three thirds).

The big southern stables of **Charlie Hills** and **Richard Hannon** each had a winner last year and should be highly competitive again (Hannon also had three places last year), while Newmarket

trainers to watch include **George Boughey** (two thirds last year to go with his two winners in 2022) and **Charlie Fellowes**, who has a notable strike-rate with three winners and four places from just 29 runners since 2019.